Gifts and Strangers

MEETING THE CHALLENGE
OF INCULTURATION

Anthony J. Gittins

PAULIST PRESS
New York and Mahwah, New Jersey

Book design by Nighthawk Design.

Library of Congress Cataloging-in-Publication Data

Gittins, Anthony J., 1943–
  Gifts and strangers: meeting the challenge of inculturation/
Anthony J. Gittins.
    p. cm.
  Bibliography: p.
  ISBN 0-8091-3088-2: $7.95 (est.)
  1. Catholic Church—Missions.   2. Missions—Theory.
3. Christianity and culture.   I. Title.
  BV2180.G58   1989
  266′.001—dc20
                                                         89-8738
                                                         CIP

Published by Paulist Press
997 Macarthur Boulevard
Mahwah, N.J. 07430

Printed and bound in the United States of America

This book is dedicated to
those women and men of faith
who are part of the
Volunteer Missionary Movement (VMM)
as it marks its first twenty years,
1969–1989
and it is born of the hope that
they will continue to be led
by the Spirit of God
and to inspire many
to respond to the call
to Mission.

Contents

Introduction

It has been gratifying and rather surprising to find, over the past few years, a real hunger on the part of many for an application of anthropology to theology, and especially to mission. However, since anthropology does strive to be comparative and cross-cultural, while theology is increasingly discovering the demands and rights of people from many traditions beyond the contemporary western Christian tradition, this is perhaps no more than appropriate after all.

But what is even more encouraging to me is that it is neither professional anthropologists nor professional theologians, so much as committed Christians seeking to *live out* or *incarnate* the gospel simply and radically, who are declaring this hunger. Nor are such people universally members of the traditional missionary organizations of the churches; a significant number are men and women who have discovered that to be Christian is itself to be called to mission, and that formal membership in a missionary order is by no means the only context, nor necessarily the best, from which to respond to the Christian vocation.

There seems to be a real ground swell, a "grass-roots" or "bottom-up" movement of women and men, from a wide range of the spectrum of the Christian tradition, who are seeking to address a variety of questions such as the following: How, in concrete terms, can we walk to the edges of our cultures and perhaps beyond and into the cultures of others, bringing with us what we truly value and consider to be a pearl of great price, but all the time trying to acknowledge and really respect the riches of local traditions and cultures? What precisely impels us to venture out, and to what extent might our motivations need purifying? How do we prepare to "give," and at the same time sensitize ourselves to hear what others might like to receive, or indeed be capable of receiving? Even more specifically, how might Jesus become explicit in situations which have not been without the presence and activity of God, but where people are not familiar with the Holy One of God, Jesus, the Christ, the Savior? Or again, what must characterize our fundamental attitude, as we approach others who do not share our history and of whose personal or cultural history we know nothing?

In *Gifts and Strangers* I have tried to keep questions of this general kind in mind, but not to address them formally, much less in a regimented order. Rather, the attempt here is to build up a context and an approach which might be conducive to the undertaking of mission, yet which is respectful of cultures and of persons. In fact I have multiplied the questions and scattered them liberally through these chapters, hoping to arrest the reader and call the reflective person to withdraw from the text fairly often, to ponder the living issues.

"Inculturation" is a rather fashionable term in theological circles today, but one that sometimes requires a good deal of explanation. It is often found in a group which includes such words as "contextualization," "adaptation," "incarnation," and "accommodation," and is sometimes used for or confused with "acculturation" or "enculturation," words more familiar to social scientists than to theologians. But my intention is not so much to define inculturation—and in any case there probably is no single, generally acceptable definition—as to plunge into it, to undertake it—initially and implicitly at least—throughout this book. But I can do more than leave the reader without any signposts, and I will be a little more specific. "Inculturation" is about what happens when the message of Jesus reaches the lives of particular people living in circumstances rather different from those of first century Palestine. More fundamentally perhaps, it is about the message itself, about the necessary and the contingent, the eternal and the temporal. It is also about myriad delicate issues relating to respect for others and yet commitment to Jesus, and about acknowledging where people actually are, existentially and morally, yet knowing that they are called to move, to develop, to respond and to grow. So it is about scripture and about the word, about tradition and about traditions, and much more.

But inculturation is not only about what happens to the message, any more than it is only about what happens to the recipients. It is also, and very much, about what happens to the messengers as they transmit and interpret, model and embody the good news of salvation. And this book is every bit as much about the last of these as it is about the first and second.

There are five sections, almost equal in length, and each devoted to an identifiable issue or area of concern. But they can be read in almost any order, and there could be many more such sections, since there are many unfurrowed fields and untapped resources remaining. By introducing each section with a cluster of statements and questions, I have tried to stay close to practical issues, though it is also necessary to address some of the theory and scholarship which contribute to our discussion, and perhaps to the clarification if not the resolution of such issues. Each section therefore closes with a set of references to works mentioned in the text and potentially useful for the further development of our thinking. I have limited them and tried to select the most easily available; some, however, do presuppose access to a good library. Reading is thus a supplement to the text; but so indeed is discussion.

Apart from trying to offer a helpful challenge and reflection to Christians responding to their vocation to be and to spread good news, I have tried to keep a couple of other important points in mind. In the first place, we must never forget that we go to real people living in real situations amid real problems, but that these people have real wisdom and real aspirations; to overlook these truths would lead to our patronizing others and ultimately treating them as no better than objects. Secondly, we cannot believe that the people to whom we go have been forgotten or abandoned by God. It is therefore a serious obligation of ours to discern the presence of God in their lives; and this in turn demands that we ourselves be led by the Spirit of God. As elementary as this may sound, it is not to be thought that, filled with good will and proselytizing zeal, we will be adequate instruments of the Spirit. Good will alone is shamefully inadequate; and proselytism in the strict sense—taking an initiative that belongs to the Spirit of God, and failing to respect the integrity and freedom of persons—is a dreadful sin.

Gifts and Strangers may possibly be difficult for some, in the sense that it raises unfamiliar or complex or even embarrassing issues. It may perhaps be difficult if it is interpreted simply as an attempt to infiltrate the Christian task with approaches from several disciplines not traditionally associated with theology or ministry. But I do believe that a book about the challenge of contemporary mission should at least raise difficult issues, since many attitudes and approaches of a previous era are nowadays either undermined or at least under scrutiny, and yet the way forward does not seem altogether clear or even possible. Whether we bemoan or try to deny such issues, they remain. Mission is delicate in its challenge and complex in its execution, even though the underlying imperative to love our sisters and brothers is as simply stated as ever. But as we endeavor to love we are inevitably drawn into new relationships, and other lives, and other histories and other aspirations; and the agenda which we bring *must* at some point encounter the life-experience and social context of those people into whose lives we erupt. And at that particular point each of us reaches the heart of the difficulty and the paradox of mission: personal loyalty to the saving message of Jesus, yet deep enough respect for others for us to be tentative and open, respectful and hope-filled, instrumental of salvation yet not usurpers of the place of the Savior.

I would like to offer this work to all who are trying to respond in a careful and sensitive way to the challenge of the great commission, to those who are concerned that Christian mission be conducted not in triumphalistic fashion but in the mode of servants, to whoever may feel unequal to the task and confused by its demands, and to any who nevertheless want to respond to the double invitation of Jesus, to "come" . . . and to "go."

My thanks are due to the Master and Fellows of St. Edmund's College at the University of Cambridge, England, for their hospitality and gifts to a stranger among them. It was in the creative space of St. Edmund's that these reflections took shape, and I would be delighted if they were acceptable as an appropriate response.

Thanks are also due, and most gladly given, to many students, in London and New York and Chicago, who have been life-giving to me. They have come from near and far, they incarnate many cultures, and they are gifted in so many ways. They are women and men, united in baptism and ecumenical faith, called to the ministry of word and worship, and anointed for a common mission in response to Jesus' call for liberty, freedom from oppression, and a year of favor. I hope that they and many like them will continue to search and struggle, to trust and to hope.

One

Beliefs, Values, and Behavior

Do we have any real understanding of our place in the universe? Are we aware of how much we search for meaning? How will we ever understand other people's worlds-of-meaning? Can a person involved in mission become a cultural and semantic puzzle solver?

Worlds of Meaning

The world in which we live is a puzzle. But in our day it is possible to live in *many* worlds; so it is more accurate to say that we live in the midst of *many* puzzles. And that is often confusing, sometimes exciting, and not infrequently frustrating!

Every Christian is invited to be missionary, and any missionary—or anyone who ministers on the edge of a familiar world—is challenged to be an enthusiastic puzzle-solver, and for two reasons. In the first place, the human spirit tends to be attracted by problems that require skill or ingenuity provided such problems do seem solvable; and missionaries, as psychological testing indicates, have above-average curiosity. Perhaps more importantly, however, as the missionary steps into another world, another set of puzzles are on display. But these puzzles make a different kind of sense, within a different context, to people who were living with them—in puzzlement or in peace—long before the arrival of the missionary; and if the stranger or expatriate really wants to approach people with respect, then a special kind of puzzle-solving, with unfamiliar rules and an unfamiliar outcome, *must* be undertaken.

We all search for meaning, but meaning is *encoded*—it does not come preassembled and prepackaged—and we have to crack the code if we are to make sense of the world—our own familiar world as well as less familiar worlds. Just by sitting watching two people play chess, or two teams play football, we will never "make sense" of the interaction; nor will we understand the meaning in all its subtlety unless we come to accept that there are

1

underlying rules which govern the play, and unless we find some way of learning them. And just as there are rules for games, so there are rules for behavior in society. But that does not mean that everyone keeps the rules; part of living in society is precisely the discovery of how one can disregard or break certain rules, which ones, and what punishments are likely to follow. Living in society is about learning to "play the game," not only about how to "keep the rules"; and just as no team game, especially one such as football, would be "real" unless some rules were broken and penalties incurred, so people's behavior cannot be understood unless both the rules under which they operate *and* their freedom to bend or break them are appreciated.

How, then, do we approach puzzles and cultures, people and meaning? And how might we refine our attitudes, as we walk on the "holy ground" of others' lives and traditions?

Points of View

THE ETHNOCENTRIC ATTITUDE

A very widespread attitude, but based on ignorance and insecurity, would approach other cultures with a built-in ethnocentric attitude. This is to place oneself and one's ideas, values and wisdom at the very center of the universe, to feel that one is "right," "better," "rational." Actually this is, initially at least, both natural and understandable, since, in trying to make sense of others' experience, we only have our own ideas, values and wisdom to use. So we try to "crack the code" of other people's puzzles, with our home-made system. But however understandable it may be, it is neverthe- less harmful and even deadly, and if the missionary cannot learn to modify an ethnocentric point of view, such a person should be repatriated as soon as possible; (this will not *solve* the problem, but at least it will not foist it on the "host" culture). A missionary who is not committed to learning from others is a disgrace.

The major difficulty with ethnocentrism, for those who presume to take some active role in the lives of others, is that in casting oneself as "right," "better," and "rational," there will, almost inevitably, be times when one judges others as "wrong," "worse," and "irrational." And that is not the end of it; the ethnocentric person will give birth to prejudices that spawn in the cultures of others, to the detriment of all and the diminution of the message of good news and hope. Ethnocentrism has been well described as acting in accordance with one's own values in a situation to which they are not relevant.[1]

So much for ethnocentrism itself. But questions remain, relating to our own perceptions about the imperative of mission. Do we believe that it is our business to judge others and to find them deficient? Do we believe that we are—perhaps because we come from "Christian" lands or are the beneficiaries of "civilization"—actually better than other people? Do we believe that our way of seeing things, and our values and beliefs, are intrinsically superior to the perspectives, values and beliefs of others? For if we have even a slight suspicion that we want to answer these in the affirmative, then we are tarred with the poisoned brush of ethnocentrism. And if we think that following Jesus *demands* that we judge others and see ourselves as the epitome of discipleship, then we are in acute need of conversion ourselves.

Perhaps not surprisingly, in view of the negative comments they would attract, some people try to avoid the charge of ethnocentrism by going to the other extreme and acting as though people in other cultures live in "the best of all possible worlds," echoing Rousseau's notion of the "noble savage." But this is at least as wrongheaded as its opposite, for there is nothing "noble" about disease, poverty, deprivation and exploitation, and such romanticism does not, unfortunately, reflect the real world in which we live. We certainly have to acknowledge the presence of injustice among people; and in fact, to refuse to be involved with the needy is itself a pernicious form of ethnocentrism, practiced by many who would like to think of themselves as informed liberals.

Perhaps if we simply acknowledge that we are all—necessarily, to a degree—ethnocentric and racist,[2] we will then be open to reeducation and conversion. But there is no place to hide if we deny these propensities in ourselves.

THE PESSIMISTIC ATTITUDE

A second attitude which can mark one's approach to another culture is the pessimistic point of view. Here, an incomer would say that it is impossible to make sense of the puzzle or the code of another culture's behavior, that meaning is after all subjective, and that the best one can do is observe passively. The pessimist is the kind of person who says wearily: "You can never understand the English/the Italians/the Russians," and carries such an attitude as essential baggage on every journey. This is the "Humpty Dumpty" attitude of *Through the Looking Glass,* where Humpty Dumpty says: "When I use a word, it means just what I choose it to mean." And this is nothing other than to claim that only I make sense.

It is important to acknowledge that the pessimist is not totally "wrong"; there are indeed subjective meanings, and it is certainly difficult at times to probe the meaning which other people attribute to the world. But meaning is essentially "shared conventions"; and we can *learn* to share. The pessimist can be gently led to a more realistic perception—and indeed must become more realistic, for otherwise evangelization is simply impossible. But it is possible, and surely desirable, to temper one's pessimism with the virtue of hope.

The Participant Observer Attitude

A third attitude which we can acknowledge is that of the participant observer. This is the approach classically adopted by the anthropologist, at least for about a century now. A serious student of another culture, or of the margins or outreaches of one's own, must become a participant observer if relationships are to develop and interdependence is to happen. And it is not simply a matter of arriving in some "exotic location" and pitching tent. Participant observation is by no means easy, and many people seem temperamentally unsuited to it. It is emotionally painful, intellectually demanding, and not without frustrations. Far from faulting those who are not comfortable with intensive living in another culture, I want to assert that to be able to do so is a gift, more explicitly a grace, and that some aspiring missionaries may, without any shame, discover that it is not theirs. But if not, may they courageously pray, withdraw, or both; for it seems clear that one cannot be involved explicitly in mission, unless one engages with a culture (or a sub-culture, perhaps near home) that is clearly different from one's familiar points of reference.

If all missionaries should be participant observers though, many are in fact not. To live in another culture but not to speak the language and to work assiduously at it every day; to live in an unfamiliar culture but to create and maintain one's own cultural ambience as a standard experience; to eat, dress and live on imported goods from one's own culture and not to experience the local hospitality through accommodations, food, and gifts

—all these are indications of a lack of engagement, a lack of participation. To be self-sufficient when living among and for people of another culture can be a grave insult and a clear indication of a lack of authenticity. The person who does not sense or exhibit any need to be fed, clothed, housed, or to receive gifts or services is the person who is not in relationship and with whom no strong links can be forged. To be independent and show no vulnerability is to fly in the face of the gospel which calls us to interdependence and the honest acknowledgment and sharing of our needs, as we share our resources.

A participant observer accepts indebtedness and vulnerability, and needs the people, for services and information, for hospitality and relationships. Such a one believes that the way to understand people is to experience the ways in which they train their children, learn and speak their language, reward and punish their members, treat their dead and address their maker. A participant observer believes it is possible—though difficult—for an outsider to make significant progress in the interpretation of another culture. A participant observer *knows* that Japanese can communicate with Germans, and Norwegians with Nigerians, even while accepting George Bernard Shaw's incisive point that England and America are "two countries divided by a common language."

The question is: Should missionaries be participant observers, and if so, at what cost?[3]

Preparation

DIFFERENT WORLDS—WORLDS OF DIFFERENCE

Avoiding the extremes of ethnocentrism and romanticism, and acknowledging that no one can *fully* enter another culture any more than anyone can fully enter the unique world of an individual—yet that partial communication is possible—just what can we do to prepare ourselves attitudinally for another world and its puzzles?

Language and meaning are intimately related. The fact that there are more than seven thousand languages and dialects in the world[4] should tell us something about the range and variety of meaning to be found in our small and fragile planet. There is not a single society in which the people consider themselves to be acting meaninglessly on an habitual basis—

though our own experience may sometimes cause us to wonder about ourselves! If meaning were a purely individual matter, then communication would be impossible. And the corollary is that where there is communication, there is (at least there is the *belief* that there is) shared meaning. Even when a mother and baby are engaged in babbles and gurgles, what may be meaningless to others or meaningless by certain narrow criteria is quite obviously meaningful: it is ongoing and reciprocal communication. Communication is something to do with a mutually satisfying exchange of signs, symbols, or "meaning"; and "meaning" itself is effectively shared when mutually held signals and values are exchanged.

Wherever social groups exist, there meaning is to be found. If the group judges certain beliefs or behavior unacceptable, that is, "meaningful but no longer approved" (and the processes whereby this may occur are several), it may institutionalize, stigmatize or ostracize any "deviants," thereby maintaining boundaries. "Meaning" is, as it were, a living entity within society; it may flourish, change, or die. When something becomes irrelevant or rejected, it is meaningless for a particular context and a particular person or group. The participant observer needs to be able to sift through and compare the meanings he or she attributes to various realities, and those acknowledged or repudiated by some or all of the people in the vicinity. For if meaning can be said to be "the shared interpretations of individuals in groups, as applied to external phenomena," then it becomes important for the missionary to be able to determine a given world-of-meaning and its inhabitants, if dialogue is not to become monologue and good sense is not to translate as gibberish.[5]

If worlds-of-meaning are "socially constructed" worlds (and we will examine this notion more fully later), then who decides who is "deviant," "irrational," "meaningless"? Clearly, an outsider is in no position to declare on the subject, though the temptation may sometimes be overwhelming! For the unassimilated outsider is perceived to be outside the world-of-meaning of the "meaning-sharing group," and therefore likely to speak much that is meaningless, including any negative judgments. It is as frustrating for well-intentioned missionaries trying to tell people what they *should* do and not do, as it must be for the audience who hear an apparently intelligent human being speaking what can only be interpreted as meaningless injunctions! The church and missionaries, as well as civil society and psychiatrists or the judiciary, have often tried to decide who is "deviant"; and if their sanctions are strong and effective, they may believe they have succeeded. But time will tell, and today many missionaries as well as many psychiatrists are a good deal more tentative in their approaches, and unsure about their "successes." We may force people to change their behavior, and we may threaten them with punishment or even damnation; but we *cannot* effectively change people's beliefs or alter their worlds-of-meaning other than with patience and time and the perceived relevance of our ideas as assimilated by the hosts.

INTRODUCING RATIONALITY

Preparation therefore implies that we begin to question our own world-of-meaning and see how it is constructed and maintained, lest we trample on others'. But we must also look beyond meaning, to rationality; for we may accept that other people attribute meaning to life and yet deny that they are rational in so doing. Are not our mental institutions full of people, many of whom attribute meaning to their actions, yet who are still "known" to be irrational? Here, indeed, is the rub. Mental illness, as the west has "constructed" it, is arguably the outcome of a set of irrelevant but strongly supported and sanctioned ideas, foisted by the "sane" on the "insane." Perhaps the "reality" is that the "sane" are crazed and the so-called "insane" are rarely any threat to themselves or each other, but only to the psychiatrists! Without pursuing this notion, we would do well to note how differently people with mental illness are treated in different cultures and through history. The so-called "developing world" seems to have a much greater tolerance for, and be much less threatened by, its less socially aware and productive members than does the mighty west. We can learn something valuable here, and apply it to our preparation for ministry in unfamiliar milieux.[6]

RATIONALITY, RELEVANCE, AND CULTURE

Although *everyone* is capable of acting unsystematically or irrationally, *no survivable group acts irrationally for long;* the cost is, quite simply, death. This implies that whichever groups survive are basically rational, systematic, predictable, orderly, and so on. If the survival of a group does indeed demand rational behavior for most of the time, then rather than looking to the putative irrationality in other cultures, we would do well to examine the contemporary "nuclear mentality" in some of the world's cultures, and ask if it is compatible with survival. Is it basically rational? Cultures litter the sands of time, destroyed sooner or later by irrational, ungrounded, unrealistic behavior.

Because rationality is related to the communication of ideas and the organization of behavior, it would seem to have some objective status, and not be simply a subjective matter. To "live in a world of one's own" is to be judged lacking in social integration and communications skills, such as would be classified as irrational activity. "Autism" describes a world totally centered on the self, lacking external points of reference and unreachable by others. But rationality bespeaks social life, and social life bespeaks rationality. So it should be possible for people to discover and utilize rationality, even though it is not primarily their own. In other words, we might accept that in other worlds and other societies, other people—apparently different from ourselves in terms of rationality—are not irrational simply because they seem to project "meaningless" behavior or belief, and that their worlds-of-meaning are viable and worthy worlds which contain the key to alternative forms of rationality.

This is dangerous ground we tread on, but as missionaries we *must* search for objective rationality in the lives of others. We must look at its context and at the rules by which it operates. Otherwise *we* act irrationally in assuming our communications will and should be understood, or in naively believing that real dialogue can characterize our attempts at evangelization.

It should now be quite clear why some missionaries are perceived as *irrelevant;* they have not allowed themselves to be contextualized within the frames of reference operated by the people. They assume that their own frames of reference are obviously the right ones, or the only ones. But since the people lack these particular frames—and have others appropriate to their needs and purposes—they can hardly be expected to pin new ideas onto them. Instead, the new ideas are fitted against the prevailing frames of reference. And if, as often happens, they do not "fit," they are relegated to the category marked "irrelevant."

Of course missionaries may be quite subtle in creating dependency on the part of the people, in such a way that though many aspects of the missionary message cannot be matched to the frames of reference of the people, some can. Thus people in the past may have fitted tobacco or education, pills or prestige, into their frame of reference, and on balance have been prepared to congregate in church or work through preparation for baptism in order to maintain the flow of goods or services. But since we cannot change beliefs as easily as we might change behavior, there was inevitably a huge discrepancy between the people's (enthusiastic) response at the behavioral level, and their perceived (lukewarm) "faith-response."

This is true where the missionary notions did not fit with the world-of-meaning of the local people. But it is not to say that change cannot happen. And it is certainly not to deny that grace can abound. Yet even grace builds on nature. And without a firm grounding in knowledge of human nature in cross-cultural contexts, mission is bound to fail at the level where it most urgently wants to succeed: the level of the heart and spirit. If Christianity is perceived as irrelevant, whose "fault" is it? And if there is no fault on the part of the missionary but simply an honest rejection—or lack of integral assimilation—by the people, must not the missionary, out of respect for individuals and consciences, withdraw if that it what the message of the people is saying?

Meaning and rationality are crucial factors in any definition of culture. Every culture carries the weight of meaning which its members give it, and which new members receive from it through their early education and "socialization." If something is meaningless to me, it can hardly be part of my culture. Now, in a pluralistic culture such a statement can easily be contested, but in a smaller-scale, more tightly-bounded culture, it is virtually a truism. What *does* a helicopter mean among Kalahari Bushmen? What "meaning" does a refrigerator or air-conditioner have for a Netsilik Eskimo? And when we come to the issue of evangelization it should now be clearer that unless Christianity finds appropriate ways and suitable categories, it cannot be understood, will never become meaningful, and is therefore never able to be assimilated in such a way that it can be catalytic for change, or a means of *metanoia*. Missionaries may try to make "them" more and more like "us"; but quite apart from this being unrealistic and conceited, it is not—dare I assert?—God's will. For God, it appears, wants each person to be more fully alive and more fully human and more fully responsive, not in the image of "us" but in the image of "God." Yet those missionaries who resist the temptation to direct the pace and shape of change in the lives of others are often at a loss for a policy and a method.

Let there be no fudging of the issue; the gospel *is* about changing people. But who is the agent of change? And what is the preferred kind of change? And what kind of change is creative and liberating as opposed to forced and enslaving? We need far more than "good will"; good will has often been the kiss of death in the history of cultures and interaction. Good will can so easily mask a patronizing, doctrinaire, elitist attitude. Good will is no substitute for good preparation.[7]

Procedure

BELIEF AND BEHAVIOR

Assuming that we acknowledge the need for rigorous preparation, the practical question is: How do we actually get started? So perhaps we can consider not so much a specific program as a number of issues that need to be addressed. The first one is the relationship between belief and behavior.

Ideally, behavior clarifies belief and belief is manifest in behavior. So ideally the study of one should illuminate the other, and both should be considered crucial. People don't just behave for no reason, and they do not have "beliefs" or believe things in a way which is totally unrelated to the world of action. If they did, then something would become irrelevant very quickly, and as we noted before, irrelevance is not compatible with a healthy, integrated existence; and so sooner or later some pathology would occur, or the individual would slough off whatever had become irrelevant.

But that is by no means all; there is a crucial element which I have not mentioned, and without which we can make no real sense of behavior or belief. For example, I may see a person putting a tooth under a pillow (behavior). I may inquire why, and receive an answer (belief), either directly or from a third party. But in order for me to draw any valid conclusions about the *meaning* of what I have experienced, it is necessary for me to pay attention specifically to the "actor" and to the "informant." So much hangs on this. If the person putting the tooth under the pillow is a six year old girl, that may or may not be significant; as a total outsider I may not know at this stage, and may need further clarification. And, likewise, if the person is the archbishop of Chicago, that may—or, indeed, may not; we do have to be open-minded!—have a bearing on the interpretation! If the "informant" is my five year old nephew, that too might have a bearing on the meaning of what is going on, but if the information comes from a shaman in a sub-Saharan village, the whole drama might take on a completely new meaning.

The crucial issue, therefore, is the *context*. Only within a specific context can the meaning be extruded from the behavior and the belief. Yet so often we wander into unfamiliar contexts and try to interpret behavior and belief with no understanding of the context—and perhaps not even thinking that context can change meaning.[8]

I may stand outside a door and overhear a voice saying: ". . . and the big bad wolf said: 'I'll huff and I'll puff and I'll blow your house down.' " If it is my sister telling her child a story, there will be no "problem." If it is the President of the United States sitting alone on the floor, there may well be! Context is crucial.

The procedural method for missionaries trying to understand people's beliefs and behavior is to situate them within the total social context. This can only be done by painstaking and informed work. Even when we think we have specified the context, we have to be aware of the fact that people do not always maintain a perfect "fit" between their beliefs and their behavior. Far from it. It is not easy to discover just what a person—let alone "the English" or "the Maasai"—believes. Do we ask individuals and then believe what they say? Even our questions are loaded in terms of what *we* think is appropriate and relevant. And even when we can get two people to agree, it is often an agreement to our formulaic way of putting things, and it is still not correct to assume that they each accept or believe in the same way.[9]

We may assume that if people "have" beliefs, they will be able to formulate them. But for the majority of people now and through history, "belief" as such was not codified or is not deemed a relevant category. It is simply not true that to be a Hindu or a Buddhist or an adherent of any number of religions, one has to have a set of beliefs that can be articulated in a formal way. Judaism, for example, sets much greater store by how one behaves than by what one believes in a formal way. And religion is much more than belief; it is coordinated social action, too. We are all familiar with people who *say* they believe certain things, but whose behavior totally belies such a statement. The scriptures are full of examples of the "lack of fit" between what people say and what they do, and Vatican II touches this point:

> The split between the faith which many profess, and their daily lives, deserves to be counted among the more serious errors of our age. . . . Let there be no false opposition between professional and social activities on the one part, and religious life on the other.[10]

Clearly we are looking here at the way "the rules," so to speak, governing belief and behavior, can be identified, and at the same time may be broken. The missionary in another culture must be sensitive not only to the breaking of rules, but to the reality of the rules themselves.

Belief Systems

Belief systems may not be available in leather-bound display copies or set in rhetoric or creeds; but that is not to say they do not exist. They can be reconstructed by the careful observer rather as from alien speech it is possible to construct a grammar, even though none of the speakers has ever seen a grammar or learned a grammatical rule. But if the missionary or anyone else is ignorant enough to assume—or, worse, to proclaim—that "these people have no beliefs (no religion, no morality)," it is a sad reflection not on the people but on the judger.[11] Unfortunately such judgers, throughout history, have tended to have authority, or certainly power to reinforce their prejudices and harm other people. It is passionately to be hoped that we ourselves will be sensitive to these matters and tread carefully as we trespass on others' lives.

Why *should* beliefs be codified? In the absence of writing, all information that is really relevant will be stored in effective ways. We overlook the great subtlety of learning in "oral" cultures (not "illiterate," since, as we shall see in Chapter Three, that is prejudicial and negative), and we ourselves, in our literate and computerized worlds of learning, have certainly lost the ability to store prodigious amounts in memory and through orally retained stories and folk-wisdom. Not only can we be confident that people living in groups will have knowledge of what their values and beliefs are, but those values and beliefs will be interrelated in such a way that we *can* speak legitimately of "belief systems." People do not have purely individual values and idiosyncratic beliefs, since they live, not in vacuums but in villages, not in tubs but in towns; that is to say they live with others, and are linked through social and other relationships. A belief system "is a scheme into which people are born (or, more rarely, construct), which helps to make sense of their own experience and to order the universe."[12]

"To order the universe"; that is very important, both to those indigenous to and those alien to a given belief system. If people did *not* have a belief system, their universe would begin to fragment. And indeed such experience is nearer to our own, where in a pluralistic world many people feel alienated and unmoored, drifting and confused, in a world with apparently no, or conflicting, values. Small-scale societies on the other hand seem to be rather better able to engage their members and prevent alienation or "anomie" (lawlessness or meaninglessness), until the outside world impinges and creates rapid and uncontrollable social change which breeds social ills of many kinds.

But belief systems, in principle, create and maintain meaning-and-order-in-the-universe. And sometimes the people under their canopy build and stoutly defend barriers and boundaries to maintain what is within and repel what is without. Not only do small-scale societies resist unwelcome encroachments from outside, but religious and other groups are entirely familiar with the process. Missionaries themselves have often been brought up in worlds whose boundaries have been sturdily built, and they are sometimes as resistant to change and as sure of their value-systems as are the people into whose worlds they walk (or indeed, fly, thus creating additional confusion!).

Belief systems are not like gentlemen's clubs or credit cards; you cannot belong to several or multiply your collection more or less at will. Emile Durkheim spoke of beliefs as "obligatory," in the sense that they existed before we did, and we are not really free to switch. An analogy might be with our own language. Few of us are bilingual (and, incidentally, even those who are raised bilingually, show marked traces of imperfections in *both* languages, when compared with their monolingual peers), and we adopt and acquire the language of our group. Later in life, we continue with that language, and indeed it is the only language there is, until we move out of the group or until the group is infiltrated. In the contemporary world almost everyone knows of other societies and other languages; but only a few centuries ago—and in rural Europe it is still often the case—people spoke one language, lived in one, enclosed world, subscribed to one belief system, and gave little thought to the nature of belief or the multiplicity of worlds.[13]

We should remember that there are still many communities that continue to resist external pressures, and a few that remain virtually homogeneous. Yet the world *is,* if not a global village, then a global metropolis or slum, and several belief systems can and do coexist, much to the confusion of the inhabitants. The existence of alternative—or conflicting—belief systems in a particular society is a crucial variable for determining the "openness" or "closedness" of that society to change. And when missionaries or others arrive at or work in particular societies, they would do well to note how "open" or "closed" the society is, and assess their own potential relevance accordingly.[14]

If belief is not to be found full-blown on every lip, or unequivocally in hallowed writings, it is alive and well in ritual and ceremonial. Ritual has been described as that form of symbolic action which redefines and re-creates boundaries, while ceremonial is used to maintain and strengthen them. So an initiation ceremony—in exotic places or as exemplified in sacramental confirmation—may be seen as a ritual, where a Sunday liturgy among believers is a ceremonial. But of course these things themselves can be misconstrued, and perceived to be what they are not designed to be. So by examining and learning to interpret ritual and ceremonial *in context,* we may learn more about belief systems. Both ritual and ceremonial try to "say the unsayable" or "do the undo-able"; they use symbolic action, *not* ignorant practical action. Magic too, contains much symbolic action, but is not only "instrumental" in action, it is also "expressive." We should examine these ideas and terms.

In the eucharist, we try to do what Jesus did, and we also try to create community. To the extent that both of these things are impossible without special assistance, the eucharistic liturgy tries to "say the unsayable" and "do the undo-able." And with a little thought we could multiply examples. Carrying a white flag in battle may symbolize the wish to surrender (and we would hope that it is so interpreted by the adversary!); lighting a fire under a pile of sticks is a practical way to prepare to cook a meal. In ritual and ceremonial it will be important for the observer to determine what the *actors* believe themselves to be doing—symbolic, or practical action, or perhaps a mixture—and not simply to assume we intuitively understand the activity. People can very easily dismiss or ridicule the action of a medicine man or other ritual specialist, because they judge it to be poor or ineffective practical action; perhaps it is nothing of the kind, but symbolic action, the significance of which is totally lost on a prejudiced observer. It is far too easy to scoff at a rainmaker, either when no rain comes, or when the rain which follows is perceived by the cynical observer to have been "in the air" anyway; it is rather more demanding and appropriate for the observer to appreciate that the rainmaker's action is far more subtle, loaded with symbolic meaning, and concerned both with "midwifing" or bringing to birth something which is indeed on the way, and acknowledging and giving thanks to a beneficent and interested creator.

This exemplifies well enough, our distinction between "instrumental" and "expressive" behavior. If the "rainmaker" were indeed trying desperately to "make rain," then his behavior might be called instrumental behavior. But if it were rather an act of obeisance and thanksgiving to the provider of rain, such activity could be called expressive behavior. It might, of course, be a mixture.[15]

Belief systems, then, are certainly not figments of the imagination; and people who act systematically are doing so as an extension—perhaps sometimes a flaunting or a travesty—of a belief system. But behavior *cannot* be understood according to the intuitions of the outsider; and simply because it makes little or no sense to the outsider is absolutely no valid reason for concluding that it makes no sense. Here are a couple of examples: If you see a man lying in a hammock, clutching his belly and claiming to experience the symptoms of pregnancy—and if the rest of the group concur in this interpretation—do you conclude that he is mad? disturbed? faking? correct? And if you lived with people whose men deliberately created nose-bleeds on a regular basis, or cut their penises with a sharp instrument and bled copiously, would you judge this to be irrational behavior? Both of these—and many, many more—are institutionalized, systematic, culturally integrated behaviors, which are not aberrant and which *do* make sense; but not necessarily in a boardroom or on Broadway, in a seminary or in a park. Context is all, in such matters as these.[16]

We will look later at language, but note here that it is virtually impossible to understand belief systems at first hand unless we know the language. For language and behavior and belief are all intimately related. A cultural heritage is transmitted through language. Through language people can convey to their young, and to each other, abstract notions, allusions, and so on, as well as prepare them for the future. But language is not a simple vehicle for the communication of ideas; the nature of reality itself is mediated to us through language in such a way that we might say our thought itself is determined by language. We could say much more than that, and will broach the subject later, in Chapter Three, but here we may imagine and ponder on the world as it exists and might be perceived by three people, all monolingual, one of whom speaks English, another Welsh, and a third Mende, a language of West Africa. Do they live in the same "world"? Do they think the same things, or in the same way? *Can* the English speaker understand "witchcraft," or the Welsh speaker "the House of Representatives," or the Mende speaker "Sheepdog Trials"?

Languages not only relate in a special way to each "world"—do African Touaregs have a word for "bus stop," or Mende people a word for "snow"?—but also symbolize the universe for people; they can express notions of "honor" and "shame," "beauty" and "ugliness," "good" and "bad" (but not necessarily in these neatly balanced categories), as well as "fearsome," "admirable," "legitimate" and the rest. So strong is language in molding our thought that its forms, through symbol and objectification, can serve *as* reality: "this *is* a good thing to do"; "that *is* a good idea"; "you *are* a liar"; "she *is* right."[17]

A question to carry with us from this section might be: are people *free* to switch beliefs? And as we address this question we acknowledge the implications it carries for evangelizers.[18]

FROM BELIEF TO ACTION

If, as we said, belief normally issues in action, and action illustrates belief, then we have to be sensitive both to the cases which exemplify a healthy relationship between the two, and cases which illustrate some pathology. But by now we will be sensitized to the fact that *we* are not univocally the ones to decide and to judge and to classify.

It is helpful to distinguish the "ethos" in which people live, from the "world view" they hold. Let me speak of the "ethos" as the palpable experience of life as it is lived. When I walk into a convent or a courtroom, a mosque or a marketplace, I immediately experience the ethos, the ambience, of the place, as something distinctive from and indeed comparable to others. But as yet I do not know whether this represents what the frequenters of such places perceive to be "good" or "bad," "normal" or "abnormal." If I think of a "world view" as representing what one perceives to be an underlying system or reality, the way things should be if everything were running smoothly, then I will have something to compare to the ethos. The convent may be in revolt, and the courtroom in uproar; the mosque may be abandoned and the marketplace out-of-season. But somewhere there are people who know how these things *should be* and *could be,* given certain modifications. In other words, there is perceived to be a set of criteria which exist—perhaps [only] in someone's mind—but are not in force. The world view could be understood as that underlying set of criteria: the way we believe things *should be* and *could be,* if everything were actually running perfectly.[19]

So long as people have a world view, even though matters are in some disarray and people break rules and commit sins, the world is not totally chaotic, because there are criteria that can still be striven for. But if chaos does set in, this is tantamount to saying that the world view has been destroyed: there are no remaining points of reference and the disarray is permanent.

Where belief and action are not in phase there is tension, call it unrest, sin, disobedience, lawbreaking and so on. If there are effective sanctions and means of enforcement all of these can be remedied, or at least people can continue to believe that there is hope. But when a real revolution occurs—civil, scientific, religious and the rest—then "belief" and "action" become quite separate. What used to be done is now *meaningless* or no longer *relevant,* and previous sanctions are no longer effective or maintained. Human history is the history of revolutions and changing world views. It is traumatic but not totally disastrous. In fact changing world views are "necessary" if "progress" is to be maintained.

All well and good. But what if certain societies are not geared for "progress" and do not perceive "change" as self-evidently "a good thing"? What if change *is* catastrophic, and people move from a world of meaning to a world of meaninglessness in a few years or a generation? What then happens to them, when their points of reference are uprooted or obscured and their ethos can in no way be reconciled with their world view? Such is the situation experienced by an enormous number of societies in this twentieth century. Is it any wonder that their behavior and beliefs appear to be disconnected if not permanently severed?

Pathological social situations *do* indeed exist. And more and more, social change is so rapid and so widespread that if missionaries are not as hard-headedly realistic as they are well-intentioned, then any naive romanticism may lead them to perpetuate situations of great pain for the people they claim to serve, rather than providing real moral support and meeting the real needs of those in distress and bewilderment. It is not sufficient either to assume that people caught in the maelstrom of social change can fend for themselves, or to assume that since they are so clearly in need they must need what *we* have decided is appropriate. A drowning person will cling to almost anything, even to the agent of his or her death. We missionaries must do better than throw out lifejackets and then expect the survivors to be unconditionally grateful to us for their rescue. Missionaries and local people together must come to integrate our lives, personally and communally, drawing beliefs, values and behavior into closer harmony, and striving for a closer fit between the ethos in which we live, and an underlying world view. However, because we missionaries and the people we encounter inhabit—in significant ways—different universes, we cannot assume too readily that what's sauce for the goose is sauce for the gander! But again, this draws us close to trouble, because as missionaries we do not want to become naive relativists and too readily endorse multiple worlds of meaning as we bring a universal message of salvation. So we certainly need some further provisions.

TRANSLATION—OR BETRAYAL?

Traditor traductor: "traitor [is] translator." Is it not true, in social or religious as much as in linguistic terms, that many things are "lost in translation," and that if we try to "translate" the gospel into other cultural contexts, it must inevitably be at the price of impoverishment or compromise? If we only look for pathologies, we might miss the fact that not all change has to be bad change, and indeed much that remains *unchanged,* in the sense of unattended to or uncared for, actually goes bad. If we overlook the potential of change for bringing good, we might also overlook the potential of translation for bringing clarification. To say in English that a person is "at death's door" is no doubt vivid and informative. And that cannot be crudely translated into French. But the French phrase *A deux doigts de la mort,* while saying something rather different, is surely no less vivid and informative. To be "two fingers away from death" is, at least to the whisky drinker, perfectly clear! And if we were to consider not only what is "lost in translation" but what may be "found in translation," then perhaps we would have a more positive basis on which to approach different cultures-in-context, and construct local theologies.[20]

Translation may very well be betrayal, if done carelessly or without respect or knowledge. Persuading local people against their better judgment to bring their drums into church in order to "inculturate" the liturgy may be embarrassing for the people and ultimately disappointing for the expatriate, unless some sense of appropriateness informs such a move. And pandering to novelty through misguided romanticism may alienate the very people we are presuming to assist. Perhaps the local people do *not* want to parade fetchingly in outmoded "native dress," any more than they wanted to cover a healthy nakedness when forced to do so; perhaps they are aspiring to other values. And uninformed missionaries may very successfully antagonize their parishioners, and then wonder why they are not receiving cooperation! No, authentic translation—of ideas, words, gestures and aspirations—is a complex issue which can only be approached along the path of communication.

To translate something from English into French, I must know *both* languages well. Yet so often people attempt "cultural translation" with little or no knowledge of one of the cultures involved. An oft-recounted example will serve here. Someone, evidently not fully conversant with English, translated Matthew 26:41, which in the Latin reads: "spiritus quidem promptus est, caro autem infirma." But instead of producing "The spirit is willing but the flesh is weak," the translator tried bravely but failed: for, missing the context, the creditable "The wine is agreeable but the meat stinks" certainly did lose something—and gained something, too—in translation!

For us, the practical and crucial question to address is how gospel-values, as well as the actual words of the scriptures, can be translated adequately, appropriately, and creatively.

THE PROBLEM OF BIAS

Bias comes in many shapes and sizes and names. Ethnocentrism, racism, sexism, clericalism—the list of forms of prejudice is not a short list. Here it is appropriate to acknowledge *personal* and *cultural* bias, which we would hope to minimize by a constant questioning of ourselves and an openness to receive and interpret feedback from others. The less comfortable we are with ourselves as learning, vulnerable, culpable human beings, the more prejudiced we will become, in an effort to cover up and appear in control.

Missionaries of a certain style are particularly prone, not only to interpret others through their own familiar categories (as we noted earlier, this is a common form of self-defense), but to harden this attitude until it becomes fixed, judgmental, and very un-Christ-like. Learning to become vulnerable, after years of learning the opposite, is tedious and painful. But if we missionaries are not vulnerable, then real communication is hardly possible; people don't "relate" to, but tend to be intimidated by, figures in shining armor, looking for trouble!

Perhaps we can glimpse ourselves through the mirror held up in these two quotations of and about sociologists and anthropologists:

As long as the idea [that the nineteenth century world was the pinnacle of human achievement] dominated, it was very hard to see the greatness in other cultures. [Even] in our own century it was still taken for granted by most people that an enormous distance separated the "primitive" from ourselves and primitive religion from ours. We can no longer believe in a gulf. But the "true equality" varies with who describes it. An old bias has been overcome, but certain ethnocentricities, or rather "culturocentricities," remain. We cannot say that now the universality of [humanity] has been established.[21]

And here is a powerful statement, worth several readings:

To see ourselves as others see us can be eye-opening. To see others as sharing a nature with ourselves is the merest decency. But it is from the far more difficult achievement of seeing ourselves amongst others as a local example of the forms human life has locally taken, a case among cases, a world among worlds, that largeness of mind, without which objectivity is self-congratulation and tolerance a sham, comes.[22]

It might be useful for us to ponder the question: Is there any value at all in personal and cultural bias? Would a total lack of bias make us less than human because apathetic and passionless? Would a lack of bias, assuming that were possible, lead to rampant relativism: "anything goes," "one thing is as good as the next"? Is bias perhaps helpful insofar as it reminds us of a hierarchy of values, judgments, truths?

Patterns and Possibilities

"RULE-GOVERNED CREATIVITY"

Ferdinand de Saussure (1857–1913), the Swiss pioneer of structural linguistics, pinpointed the unobvious but blindingly clear fact that in spite of the amazing creativity of language, underlying it is a *discoverable* and *describable* structure, largely unnoticed by the speakers. Noam Chomsky (1927–) extended the Saussurean revolution and reduced contemporary English to some one hundred and fifty rules for creating, assessing and judging "utterances" as grammatically acceptable. The possibilities opened up by linguistic studies this century are enormous, for missionaries as well as for linguists. For perhaps it is possible to discern "rules" underlying behavior as well as language, and to determine the criteria by which to assess whether any given example is "behaviorally" or "grammatically" acceptable.

But, for missionary purposes, we have two main problems. In the first place, can we visualize a moral universe with several or many different "grammars," and would not this conflict violently with a single gospel truth and a single right way of living? (And if there *is* deemed to be only one legitimate moral and doctrinal "grammar," it is not difficult to see what a scramble there would be [there already *is*!] among missionaries of many tongues, to propose their own version!) And secondly, even if by some eventuality we could conceive of and agree upon a single, universal "moral and doctrinal grammar," our problems are not over. Chomsky himself formulated the brilliantly grammatical, winsome, but *meaningless* "sentence," "colorless green ideas sleep furiously," to show some of the limitations of grammar without a built-in semantic component which would check grammatical constructs against the real world of meaning. The well-known "The wine is agreeable but the meat stinks" is another form of utterance which seems perfectly grammatical but somehow fails to convey an intended meaning.

So, back we come to meaning. And meaning needs context. Two chess-players are in *communication* when they play. Though they use the same set of rules, each plays differently, and plans are made and adapted according to the opponent's actual play, but also according to each competitor's perceptions and interpretations, intuitions and guesses, during the actual play. Communication is *not just* "playing by common rules," which is why chess, with its myriad moves and endless possibilities, is so compellingly interesting.

Now I say all this about chess, but I am a non-chess-player! I just know the basic rules, but not the strategies or game-plans. Yet still I can validly speak about chess as comprehensible, *because* it is "rule-governed" and also *because* it permits creativity and even rule-breaking, to the smart or unscrupulous! And, given time and motivation, I could come not only to learn the rules, but actually to feel comfortable in applying them. But still my creativity would be much slower in coming. It was years ago, when I lost predictably to a virtual toddler, that I gave up, even though both of us knew, and ostensibly used, the same set of rules!

Carrying the chess and the linguistic analogies back to the subject of mission, what can we say? Each culture "plays a different game," but with rules which are *discoverable* and *describable*. If we are to understand, we *must* discover and learn the rules. Rules from other contexts simply will not apply, any more than the grammatical rules for Bulgarian will allow us to produce good Italian. In fact, rules from the wrong context will be disastrously misleading.[23]

BREAKING THE RULES

If rules do not change, and if nobody breaks them, then we have a "steady state" system. But neither games nor languages work like that for long. And certainly cultures and people do not, in spite of numerous efforts to make them do so. If we consider social institutions such as state or church, we can see the tension that exists between the law makers or law preservers on the one hand, and the law keepers or law breakers on the other. The process of change will be painful, and yet change does and must come, for where there is no change there is no life, and societies, languages and people that do not change die.

People who live in "traditional" societies do not perceive change as a good or a necessary thing, and the whole effort of society is focused on claiming and recreating the past, and on stability. Yet in spite of people's perceptions, even "traditional" societies do change, from stone axes to steel knives, from gourds to plastics, from breech-clouts to Levi's; and soon there are transistors and headache pills, Nestlé's Baby Formula and brassières, Mercedes trucks and submachine guns.

And there are more traumatic ways to break the rules. The very presence of mission or other outside agencies provides a new range of opportunities and alternatives; and once these exist, people begin to remake their choices. Sometimes the choices are manifest in the repudiation or the overthrow of what is not wanted. But we need to discover what the people themselves perceive as deviant, objectionable or intolerable; otherwise we will be totally confused about where the underlying rules are, and what constitutes deviance rather than chaos. Societies have a built-in tolerance (higher or lower from one to another) of rule-breakers, as well as a theoretical breaking point which, once reached, signals the breach between the ethos and the world view. But rule-breaking may be a necessary procedure for drawing attention to coming change.

One of the traditional missionary approaches was the "Clean Sweep," which attempted to eradicate everything within a target culture, in order to replace it with something new. But if you deliberately sow the seeds of chaos, there is simply nothing permanent which can be grafted onto new stock. Demoralized and disillusioned people can hardly turn around to those responsible and accept them with trust and hope. If you forbid me to speak in my language when I do not know yours, how will I ever learn it?

A very serious question which now arises is this: Do missionaries try to change people? But since I have already answered this for myself, and called for an honest acknowledgement of the impact of the gospel and a sincere effort to repudiate naive romanticism, the question can be reformulated to inquire more specifically: *How* might the missionary approach the delicate and fraught issue of change, social and theological?

MODELS AND MUDDLES

If it is possible to interpret other people's behavior after the fact, is there any way of understanding it before it actually happens? Though it would be very helpful to think we could predict the behavior of others and understand its rationale, we have to acknowledge human freedom and unpredictability, lest we reduce people to automata and get totally muddled by our models.

Though we may not predict any given piece of behavior with accuracy, since people differ and change their minds, nevertheless we can approach others with some expectations of comprehension. Our linguistic or game analogy helps us again, because we know that we will be able to gauge whether a response to our statement or a move on the chess board is "legitimate," "fair," "meaningful," or "illegal," "improper" or "meaningless." If an interlocutor responds to us in gibberish, or a chess opponent eats the pawn, we *know* something "deviant" is happening. And the knowledge upon which we base that judgment is the same body of knowledge that tells us how a person "might" or even "should" act. And in that sense, there can be real predictability of other people's responses.

Like the linguists, we missionaries need to work toward the production of "generative models" which will account for behavior within the framework of its own cultural grammar, and which will understand it as meaningful or not, on its own terms and not on ours. To do any less, as a preparation for evangelization, is to fail to show simple respect to other people. In a remarkably widely-read and widely quoted book, Vincent Donovan brings this dimension of the missionary task vividly alive.[24]

Every utterance presupposes a language, every game presupposes rules, every ethos presupposes a world view, and every piece of social behavior presupposes an underlying social structure. As missionaries we have to be cultural and semantic puzzle-solvers, because every language and game, every ethos and piece of behavior is *coded;* and we do not set off with all the codes. With patient effort we can build some helpful models, but unless we work through the swamps and the muddles, we will never reach the dry ground when our models can be assembled as viable structures.

Postscript

Just as language is finite and exists within real communities, so with culture and meaning. The missionary task, then, is enormous. We may learn *about* another culture or set of meanings from third parties, but we can only "learn culture" and "learn meaning" from direct experience. Each person thus carries the responsibility for creating and experiencing, bungling and cherishing, communication; it is not something that just happens or something that exists in culture, like palm trees and mud-huts.

Listen to José Comblin trying to put this into words:

It is the Church [who, precisely?] that receives the words expressed by Jesus in human form as signs of God's word and message. It is the Church that tries to find the words capable of touching human hearts. In short, it is the Church that performs the constant task of mediation and translation. Real transmission of God's word entails a constant reinvention of the message so that it will accurately express the substance of the divine word to human beings. The message does not exist on its own as some fixed, prefabricated discourse, as some standing monument of the past, as a textbook for recitation. The message is a "wayfaring" one, calling for translation at every moment.[25]

"Structuralism" is a way of thinking about the world. It accepts that the world is not composed of totally discrete entities but that *relationships* are the building-blocks of meaning. No experience or thing can be adequately understood without the context or structure in which it is embedded. And, similarly, structures can only be understood as composites, a change of any of whose parts will produce a different structure. So the gospel somehow must be brought to the structures and relationships that characterize people's lives, just as those structures and relationships must bow responsibly —not cower, and not be forced—before the truly relevant revelations of Jesus.

Comblin says it is "the church" that transmits the message of Jesus; but "the church" ultimately means people. Evangelization may indeed be what "the church" does, but its shape and effects depend, at least in part, on you and me. As I use it throughout this book, evangelization is intended to be understood at its most simple and etymological: the announcing of the good news of Jesus in a comprehensible way, in the hopes of its being welcomed. But this depends on its being understood. My assumption is that if it is indeed announced appropriately, its relevance will be discernible by the recipients. If it is not perceived as relevant, that might be due to the inadequacy of the messengers or the perceived untimeliness of the message; for evangelization does not of itself absolutely guarantee the wholehearted acceptance of the message, but works with the gratuitous grace of God to produce a response in the hearers.

But evangelization, if it is adequate, must go hand in hand with the building of relationships, because relationships define the church as a community of believers, and are a necessary part of the context in which conversion of heart takes place: the community itself. If evangelization and the facilitation of real interdependence do not march together, the results will be dire: "proselytization" masquerading as evangelization will produce the poison of coercion and imperialism; or too casual an approach will lead to dilettantism or uncritical relativism, rather than the clear presentation of the scandal of the cross and the undertaking of serious moral responsibility. The relationships—from which true evangelization and its fruits may spring—are of course the grace of God and the living word; but they are also, as we have seen in this chapter—and to paraphrase Johann Sebastian Bach—"Well-Tempered Communication" and "The Art of Translation."

Notes and Bibliography

1. A very accessible and popular treatment is Anne Wilson Schaef's *Women's Reality: An Emerging Female System in a White Male Society*, Minneapolis: Winston, 1985; and her follow-up, especially in *When Society Becomes an Addict*, New York, Harper and Row, 1987:7–12. Schaef describes various *systems*,

and the effect of a particular form of ethnocentrism—here patriarchy, or "The White Male System."

2. Eugene Nida, *Customs and Cultures,* New York, Harper and Row, 1954, contains many helpful insights, and a section (Chapter 3) on "Race and Ranting" which is applicable for this and our next chapter.

3. For an examination of some problems and potential avenues of approach, see Peter Winch, "Understanding a Primitive Society," in Bryan Wilson (ed), *Rationality,* Oxford, England, Basil Blackwell, 1970:78–111.

4. Depending on our reference, and indeed the criteria employed, we can distinguish as many as almost seven and a half thousand, or as few as three thousand or so, different "linguistic groups." If we include the United States, Canada, Australia, South Africa, Anglophone West Africa and England, under the general category of "English speakers," the number will be lower; if we distinguished those who speak with the dialects of Somerset, Northumberland, Appalachia, South Carolina, and so one, then the number obviously increases. (And we could of course repeat such kinds of classification, in relation to "French speakers," "Spanish speakers," and the rest). Again, people may be mutually intelligible, but at less than one hundred percent, and people who ostensibly share a single language may find it quite difficult to understand each other.

5. A poignant essay on meaning is Viktor Frankl's *Man's Search for Meaning,* New York, Pocket Books, 1963.

6. For an iconoclastic view of orthodox psychiatry, and a trenchant and compelling argument, see Thomas Szasz, *The Myth of Mental Illness* (revised edition), New York, Harper and Row, 1974; and for an alternative and similarly interesting read, Michel Foucault's *Madness and Civilization,* New York, Random House, 1965.

7. Geertz maintains, rightly I think, that we (he is talking of anthropologists) need to be more than puzzle-solvers; we need to be diagnosticians too. He speaks of "a science that can determine the meaning of things for the life that surrounds them." And we cannot assume that the meaning *for others* is the same as the meaning *for us:* "most people, I am convinced, see African sculpture as bush Picasso, and hear Javanese music as noisy Debussy." *Local Knowledge,* New York, Basic Books, 1983:120, 119.

8. Mary Douglas points up some of the deficiencies of the sociology of religion, and urges a phenomenological theory, whose method "consists in setting people's beliefs back into the social context of their lives, by careful, intensive field research." In *The Active Voice,* London, Routledge and Kegan Paul, 1982:2, 9.

9. I cover some of this in an article in *New Theology Review* 3/1989.

10. Vatican II, "The Church in the Modern World," n. 43, in Walter Abbott

(ed.), *The Documents of Vatican II*, London, Geoffrey Chapman:243. See also Isaiah 58:1–12; Matthew 21:29–30; 23:3–23; Mark 7:10–13, and so on.

11. See Igor Kopytoff, "Knowledge and Belief in Suku Thought," *Africa,* 51 (3):709–723. A most helpful article, particularly on what "believers" are "believed" to "believe."

12. The quotation is from Manning, in Carol Hill (ed), *Symbols and Society,* Athens, Georgia, University Press, 1975; Frank Manning, "The Prophecy and the Law: Symbolism and Social Action in Seventh-Day Adventism," pp. 30–43; another good example of "belief-in-action" is Michael Angrosino's "The Case of the Healthy Hindu," pp. 44–57. Manning shows how religious symbols serve to synthesize a people's ethos and their world view, while Angrosino traces modifications in behavior to a search for the socially constructed values of "respectability" and "reputation," on a Caribbean island.

13. Carol Hill, in the Introduction to her edited work, *Symbols and Society,* Athens, Georgia, University Press, 1975:1–10, provides a useful survey and introduction to this general area.

14. A seminal article is Robin Horton's much discussed and gradually somewhat modified "African Traditional Thought and Western Science," which is accessible in Bryan Wilson (ed.), *Rationality,* Oxford, Basil Blackwell, 1970:131–171, somewhat abridged. The original article is in *Africa* 1967:51–70, and 155–187. An enormous amount of contemporary thinking on rationality and modes of thought can be traced to this article.

15. There is a fascinating open discussion between Clifford Geertz and Johnathan Miller in the latter's *States of Mind,* London, BBC Publications, 1983:194–210; and, incidentally another, between Miller and Thomas Szasz, pp. 272–290, called "Objections to Psychiatry." Both discussions concern the problem of how we "know" and of what happens when our "knowledge" seems very different from that of others.

16. For the "couvade" or "lying-in" of men, in Brazil, there is a learned article by Patrick Menget, "Time of Birth, Time of Being: The Couvade," in *Between Belief and Transgression,* edited by Michel Izard and Pierre Smith, Chicago, University Press, 1982. And for men who wound themselves, the book by Ian Hogbin, *The Island of Menstruating Men,* San Francisco, Chandler, 1970.

17. On the possible existence of an "innate imperative" to "learn the rules" of religious phenomena, see Anthony Stevens, "Thoughts on the Psychobiology of Religion and the Neurobiology of Archetypal Experience," in *Zygon,* 21, (1) 1986:9–29. That issue and the following were devoted to recent discoveries in neurobiology, as they relate to religion, the social sciences and the humanities.

18. A fine survey, apart from Kopytoff (note 11, above), and very readable, is John Beattie's *Other Cultures,* London, Cohen and West, 1964, Chapter 5.

19. For Geertz' treatment of "ethos" and "world view," to which I am

indebted, see his "Religion as a Cultural System," in Michael Banton (ed.), *Anthropological Approaches to the Study of Religion*, London, Tavistock, 1966:1–46, especially p. 3.

20. The notions "lost" and "found" in translation derive from an essay by Clifford Geertz in his *Local Knowledge*, New York, Basic Books, 1983. Chapter Two is called "Found in Translation: On the Social History of the Moral Imagination," pp. 36–54. Constructing local theologies is actually the title of the book by Robert Schreiter, which is very helpful, and particularly around pp. 8ff where he discusses translation models used in theology. See *Constructing Local Theologies*, New York, Orbis Books, 1985.

21. In his introduction to *Perspectives in the History of Religions*, Los Angeles, University of California Press, 1977, Jan de Vries looks at a variety of approaches to religion. This quotation is from p. xv.

22. Taken from Geertz's introduction to his *Local Knowledge*, New York, Basic Books, 1983:16.

23. An excellent and short survey of some key notions is provided by Terence Hawkes, *Structuralism and Semiotics*, London, Methuen, 1977.

24. Vincent Donovan's *Christianity Rediscovered*, London, SCM Press, 1982, is a "must" for weary missionaries, as for vigorous ones! It is the story of evangelization among the Maasai of Tanzania. Also published in New York, by Orbis Books, 1982.

25. Always compelling and often controversial is José Comblin's *The Meaning of Mission*, New York, Orbis Books, 1977. Extracts taken from pp. 33–34.

Two

Growing in Age, Wisdom, and Grace

How does an American become an American, a Briton a Briton, or a Zulu a Zulu? Could an American hope to become a Zulu, or a Zulu a Briton? What are the implications for missionaries working in other cultures? What might "conversion," "renewal" or "inculturation" entail in practical terms?

Clearing the Ground

RACE AND CULTURE

"Race" is an enormously loaded word. It has been used by so many people in so many ways that it is now perhaps more confusing than enlightening. We speak of the "many races" in the human family—peoples distinguished from others by common ancestry and named as Caucasian, Mongoloid and Negro—and of divisions of these. But we also speak frequently of "the human race" as a unity; so where do we stand? Throughout history and across cultures, people have categorized themselves, each other and their world; and insecurity perhaps more than anything else has led people to posture and to demean others while exalting themselves, on the grounds of supposed racial superiority and the consequent inferiority of others.

Race refers to certain specific *genetic* characteristics—those occurring at the microbiological level, within the chromosome—which distinguish one group from another. Quite another thing is nationality, a *social* construct; "American" may refer to those who are citizens of the United States, irrespective of their race. There is no such thing as an American gene or a British gene. And furthermore, race is not to be confused with blood, for blood-types are supra-racial and certainly supra-national, and no microscope has never seen "royal blood" or "Irish blood," in spite of popular terminology. Yet popular terminology is very pervasive and persuasive, and people who think that "royal blood" is something real and special are likely to think also that paupers or refugees or slaves—or even Jews or pagans or foreigners—have specific, and of course inferior, kinds of blood!

Some people still feel outraged or at least uncomfortable at the thought of being transfused with "inferior" blood, however they reach that racist judgment; and I well remember when, giving blood in Africa, I joked that this was really premium blood, four-star quality! It shames me to think who might have taken me seriously. But the only possible differences, apart from blood-types, are not between kinds of blood, but are to be found in characteristics carried *in* the bloodstream.'

Assuming we can accept that race is not something which divides, discriminates and ranks people hierarchically, then we are theoretically open to acknowledging the principle of the unity of humanity. If only the reality were as easily established! But to confuse such unity with uniformity would be to deny the function of culture and of cultural processes, the main topic of this chapter. I certainly want to emphasize human unity, but at the same time I must recognize variety and difference at various levels, including the cultural, otherwise there is serious danger of treating everyone exactly the same!

Culture has to do with the way people in groups interact with their environment; it has nothing necessarily to do with race. We know perfectly well that Vietnamese "boat-people" were able to adjust to the United States and grow up very differently than if they had remained in Vietnam. And if a baby born to white American parents in Chicago were to be taken to Shanghai at a very early age, and brought up there by Chinese people, that child would have not the slightest difficulty in learning Chinese and assimilating the culture.

Race is a "given," but culture is learned; and we shall examine what this means in practice, since the people we approach as Christians and missionaries are already enculturated. And though people are able, in principle, to adjust to any culture, it is nevertheless true that once a person has been incorporated into a particular culture—by the processes known as "socialization"—it is by no means easy to move into another, at least as far as mentality is concerned. Culture includes the beliefs, values and behavior of which we have already spoken, as well as whatever shared knowledge constitutes the basis of social action; and these things become such a part of our life—a sort of second skin—that we cannot simply slough them off and continue on our way.

"Given" and "learned," "race" and "culture," "nature" and "nurture":

these are complementary pairs, both elements of which contribute to the total person. But we cannot easily quantify or precisely determine the relative importance of each. A "genius" may produce a "fool," a mentally disturbed parent may give birth to a stable and balanced child, just as a man or woman with a congenital disease may parent a healthy child, or a saint give birth to a sinner. Culture plays a crucial part in socialization, but it is not the only element, any more than is heredity alone.

Now even though we, perhaps magnanimously, endorse the equality of all races and our common humanity—in spite of the real differences, whether natural, cultural, or social, that also mark us—we should record that it was not always so, and it is not necessarily so: human equality is a contingent fact of history.

We did not always believe in a universal humanity. People long interpreted the differences between them as marking fundamental disparities, and until quite recently "Christendom" or "the west" was not even close to a definition of "human." Rome, by papal bull, defined the status of those bipedal "creatures" found (as well as whoever might be found in future) by the great discoverers, only in 1537. The people of the Americas, "discovered" by Christopher Columbus more than forty years earlier, were henceforth to be considered human! This was important, since they now could, and indeed should, be baptized and saved. But it was by no means the end of the matter, for there were many more expeditions and "discoveries." Orangutans [Malay: *orang*, man, + *hutan*, forest] provoked great speculation, and as late as 1768 the president of the Berlin Academy of Sciences wrote: ". . . voyagers assure us that they have seen wild men, hairy men with tails: a species indeterminate between the monkeys and us. I would rather one hour of conversation with them than with the finest mind in Europe."[2]

Long before Darwin and the voyage of the *Beagle* in the 1830s, there was enormous interest in the nature of human nature and the specificity of humanness. But even in that enlightened age, some suggested mating an orangutan with a prostitute (in order, presumably, to "see" whether a "human" would be produced from the union), in supreme disregard of the susceptibilities of either. And still in our own day, major controversy surrounds the definition of "human" and of life itself (not to mention the definition of "definition"), a fact which should lead us to acknowledge that definitions are a function of the culture (and therefore the science, the medicine and the religion) that produces them. Yet we *can* assert that there is no such thing as a "race gene," that people the world over remain pretty much the same, and that if the nuclear age were to end in a mushroom cloud "and only the Xhosa people of the southern tip of Africa survived, the human species would still retain eighty percent of its genetic variation," which only goes to show that we are more similar than different.[3]

And, secondly, human equality is not a necessary but rather a contingent fact of history. Among our evolutionary ancestors were the australopithecines. Some of their descendants survived—among whom are the branch known as *Homo habilis*—and some did not. Among the latter was *Australopithecus robustus,* who disappeared less than a million years ago, a mere blink on the face of history. The *robustus* family were contemporaries and neighbors of *Homo erectus.* Why *robustus* disappeared is simply not known; it might have been otherwise. But had it been otherwise we might now be faced with the reality of sharing the earth with genetic cousins with a brain only a third the size of our own, and a correspondingly lower intelligence. "Would we have built zoos, established reserves, promoted slavery, committed genocide, or perhaps even practiced kindness?"[4] Or would we have tried to "civilize," "educate," "convert" or "evangelize" them? It is interesting to speculate on our putative attitudes to other (lower) forms of human life, and on our possible justifications for such attitudes. But human equality is not a *necessary* fact of history, and there are still numerous shameful instances to demonstrate that for all its theoretical acceptability, it remains widely unrealized today.

PROCREATION AND RE-CREATION

Reflecting on the rich diversity of humankind, we can both accept the uniqueness of each person *in some sense,* and yet assert that we share a common humanity. This latter is not simply a matter of "faith" or "theology," but a matter of experience for all who really look. For people *can* understand each other, and behavior *is* laden with meaning, and people *do* act rationally: communication and mutual intelligibility *are* possible, however difficult.

People do not uniquely and individually and single-handedly modify their environment, create their language and formalize their belief-systems; the world existed before us, and we are born "into" a world, in which we acquire (inherit, learn, receive) our environment, language and beliefs. But we do not simply "absorb" everything, like sponges; we are also the active agents in our genesis, and we acquire something specifically human but also very personal—sensitivity, or the development of feelings—which will mark our subsequent relationships and significantly determine our capacity to change.[5]

Once we have matured as members of our group and assimilated its rules and expectations, we become relatively ethnocentric; and if group or territorial boundaries are strong and tightly maintained, we will have little or no awareness of alternatives. There are of course cultures and groups that appear extremely open, boundary-less and accommodating to outsiders. But relatively speaking, adult members of human groups are settled in certain ways. We cannot easily think that our thought is wrong. We may of course admit error in individual cases, but the patterns of our thinking cannot be changed without pain; and the idea that our epistemological system itself may be "wrong" is one that is simply not entertained by most of us.

These notions—that human groups operate on shared conventions that allow for communication, that people are born into a world that preexisted them and that is perceived as permanent, and that it is not easy and may be impossible to think that our ways of thinking are wrong—will be of crucial importance as we consider more carefully the impact of evangelization on other cultures. They should help us understand more easily the kinds of reactions we meet, as well as the kinds of problems we ourselves pose and constitute as we "invade" other people's worlds of meaning. But in order to think through the implications of evangelization, we will have to step back and approach the whole issue of social life, not from familiar perspectives and with comfortable answers to the questions that *we* deem appropriate, but in a much more tentative and open way.[6]

Becoming Human

WHAT IS HUMAN?

"Life is sacred from the moment of conception": this is such a well-known maxim that we may take it for granted. But that is not quite enough to make it "true" or "real," whatever that might mean! What of those people who do not take it "for granted"? Are they perverse, or simply "wrong"? And if "wrong," and we tell them what is "right," why don't they change their minds? There is more to the question than first appears. Our starting point is this: the answer to the question "who is human?" will be a "socially constructed" answer, and will differ across societies, and even within a society. If this means that there is no such thing—in an absolute sense—as a "human," then we must consider the implications of that very seriously. Meanwhile, I will try to illustrate the point.

At least as far back as Romulus and Remus the heroic founders of Rome, there have been documented examples of individuals discovered in jungle or forest or the wilds, perhaps reared by wild animals. The so-called "Wild Boy of Aveyron" in 1800 is perhaps the best documented case, but there have been others like the wolf child of Hesse (1344), Wild Peter of Hanover (1724), and the Wild Boy of Burundi (1974), as well as a case in Sierra Leone in the early 1980s. Jean Jacques Rousseau, in *Emile* (1762), used the term "noble savage" in epitomizing what he believed to be the natural goodness of humankind and the warping and corroding influence of society; but society undoubtedly does mold and strengthen (whatever else it may do to corrode), so that if a child were to be reared entirely outside human society, its impairments would be severe enough for us at least to question the appropriateness of the designation "human." To be deprived of all "culture" is potentially as serious and problematic as to be deprived of all "nature" (all our genetic substance and the interrelatedness of its parts).

How, then, are such "savages" to be defined? What of the famous "elephant man" John Merrick? Of course, *we* would not dream of denying them humanity, but where does one draw the line? What is an autistic child? An anencephalic child (especially since in 1987 a live anencephalic child was used as a donor for a heart transplantation in the United States)? How do we "define" a senile centenarian, or a comatose trauma victim years after the accident? And if these are clear, then what about a live but badly deformed fetus *in utero* or a hydatidiform mole? And what possible problems could there be with a twin, or a girl baby? But many people would want to define one or other of these as not human; many societies accept without demur that they are not; and the reasons adduced are not simply "immoral" reasons, but represent honest efforts to "define" and "name" the world as it is.

Definitions come from people, and as people, environments, and conditions vary enormously, so definitions may be expected to differ, not so say undergo change. Here are a few examples. In August 1985, after three years' legal wrangling, the county of Los Angeles ruled that 16,500 aborted fetuses could be buried. They had been discovered in February 1982 in a container at the home of a man who ran a medical laboratory. The legal decision, in prescribing fetal *burial,* is stating that they should be treated as *human beings;* incineration is permissible for "non-human" tissues, but burial is mandatory for humans. There has now been a change in definitions.

Legislation is now pending in Britain which would modify the regulations governing "burial" and "disposal" by simply changing the "definitions" of unborn fetuses, according to the number of weeks of gestation.

By way of an anomalous case, I was once—at an American hospital in the late 1960s—called to anoint an amputated limb prior to its *burial,* and it was explained to me that it had to have a death certificate! Limbs are defined differently from pathological tissues or organs, and I suspect that a large part of the decision is due to intuitive or aesthetic reasons. But the situation is odd inasmuch as whoever (or whatever?) needs a death certificate has presumably enjoyed some measure of independent viability, which an amputated leg never did. And, similarly, western countries are still struggling to "define" the status of the unborn fetus, leaving many confusing situations for large numbers of people.

Among the Venda of West Africa, a newborn child lacks social significance ("humanness") until the first teeth appear. Thus, a woman's offspring is "defined" as human once it cuts a tooth; before then, since it is not human, it does not need to be treated as such! What then is "murder"?

Clear definitions serve to separate categories, but some anomalies will always remain. If you believe that, in the very nature of things, humans multiply their offspring one at a time whereas animals usually do so in multiple births, then what happens to your classification when a human mother has twins? It depends on the culture and the classification. And similarly for monstrous births. If the culture maintains that two "humans" cannot be produced by a human mother at one birth, then to kill one or both twins is not—by definition—infanticide! The Nuer of the Sudan traditionally had no great problems with anomalous births either; they simply treated monstrous births as "mistakes," as "hippopotamuses" accidentally born to human mothers, and otherwise indistinguishable from real human children. And so the remedy was simple: they returned the "hippo" to the river and left it for its real mother.[7]

Another familiar example shows how definitions are made. If we "define" a rooster as a bird that crows at dawn, then, provided we take care to strangle any such bird that crows during the night, we preserve the force of the definition, we provide food for the pot, and we maintain relatively undisturbed nights!

Finally, from the 1917 Code of Canon Law, a splendid example. Canon 748: "Monsters and strange creatures (wonders, phenomenal beings) should always be baptized at least conditionally; in doubt however, whether it is one or more human beings, one of them can be baptized absolutely, the others conditionally." This may have satisfied canonists, but not necessarily parents, not to mention the possible feelings of the aforementioned "strange creatures."

The answer to the question "what is human?" now seems much less obvious than it was; cultural definitions are rooted to the reality as experienced by the members of a culture.[8] Crossing cultural boundaries we encounter different realities, different perceptions of truth, and different definitions. As evangelizers we are committed to respecting the worlds into which we walk. This turns out to be a mighty task.

WHO IS HUMAN?

Assuming a society has some kind of working definition of who is human, it nevertheless does not follow that every individual who fulfills the formal requirements of the definition is thereby treated as equally human. Humanization is the process of making human, and "socialization" is the term often applied to specific or identifiable elements in this process. Children have to be trained, to be *made* human, to become assimilated to the society that preexisted them. They must learn what their society is, where its boundaries are, and how it relates to a wider world, to current events, history and the future. They should discover their own place and freedom, their limitations and the sanctions which govern them, and the meaning of their lives.

If socialization is about becoming human, and if it is a learning process, what about those who are incapable of learning? Will they already have been deemed "non-human," or will they be so judged when they are seen to be unteachable? Can a community accommodate those unable to learn? How does a social group look after its weaker members, at any and every stage of life? Every society must address such issues, and has certainly done so long before the arrival of a missionary. Outsiders would do well to examine local processes of socialization, the better to discover a potential "fit" between the gospel and cultures, between the socialization implicit in evangelization and that already characteristic of each social group. Without such sensitivity on the part of missionaries, the gospel will not be assimilated and conversion will not be facilitated, though something may indeed be foisted on people who may in turn evince responses which could be mistaken for conversion.

Primary and Secondary Socialization

Socialization in General

When we use the word "society" we acknowledge its objective reality: we accept that "out there" are organized groups of people who share many social institutions, including language, economic and political systems, and patterns of belief and thought. But society, somewhat like beauty, is also in the eye of the beholder; it has a subjective side. Each person must absorb impressions, make judgments, and form values, building a personal synthesis. This entails a process known as "socialization," and it is what we need to examine now, the better to understand people-in-society, especially in societies unfamiliar to us.

Through socialization a human being is individuated within a relevant group; he or she becomes a person, a member of society. But it is society itself—through traditions and sanctions and accumulated wisdom and public priorities—that makes individuals into persons and members; and that of course implies a wide variety of styles and emphases. If groups are to be perpetuated—clearly a priority—then not only must offspring be produced but they must be assimilated to the group and trained to meet its needs. And so we can say that "reality" is "socially constructed," since the child it taught what is relevant and what is not, what is to be taken seriously and what can be dismissed. Take dreams: in western society, children who have nightmares are comforted by a parent and told that they need not worry, that it was "only" a dream, and that what is not real cannot hurt. Thus a child learns that what *seems* real is not always so, and that dreams are not "real." Of course Jungian analysts and others might take great exception to such a simplistic view, arguing that dreams help in the social reconstruction of reality. But among the Hausa of Nigeria, children are taught that dreams *are* "really real" and far more meaningful than any other experiences. A child who wakes with a dream is thus *not* told that it was "only" a dream, but is helped to internalize the dream and learn its important lessons.

Reality is socially constructed, particularly during our socialization; we see, hear, and do, what our society, or a section of it, tells us to. And we do *not* see or hear or do many things, because they are not noticed or deemed relevant. We do sometimes break the rules, rules that are themselves socially constructed. And there are many experiences that simply elude us. What we are trained to perceive is what becomes the real; whatever "remainders" there may be will either pass unnoticed or be judged as unreal. Reality is mediated to us in two main ways: by training and by language. Language is the topic of the next chapter; here we look more closely at training. Though socialization occurs within specific cultures, we can actually say something of general validity; details would have to be discovered and applied to individual societies. There are, for example, two important stages for a child to negotiate: internalization and generalization.[9]

Internalization is the process whereby the external world is appropriated and made meaningful. This rather sophisticated process essentially consists of socially provided mechanisms through the use of which an infant "tames" the wild world of sense impressions. Transport a child from London to an igloo within the Arctic circle, and it will be overwhelmed and alienated. But lead it by the hand into its own familiar bedroom in Wimbledon, and it will identify and name a host of things. This particular bedroom is a meaningful world; the igloo is threatening and chaotic. Reverse the process and an Eskimo child will scream at the suburban bedroom yet gurgle in its familiar environment. As internalization is taking place, each child is learning appropriate "recipe knowledge": how to get from the bedroom to the kitchen, or from the igloo to the tundra. Recipe knowledge is simply appropriate—"how to"—knowledge: how to dress, how to eat, how to attract help, and so on. The child who learns such knowledge is acting on the world and observing the world's reaction. Relationships are modified as the child is assimilated into a stable and preexisting world and takes the first tentative steps to independence. Without internalization and recipe knowledge, the individual, whether Xhosa or Christian, missionary or Mende, is alienated or lost.

There is generalization also: the process whereby a child learns to do or not to do things, not simply because "mommy" or "grandpa" says so, but because certain things simply should or should not be done. The process may be like this: first a child learns "*Mommy* does not like you to bite your *sister*"; later it will generalize to "*I* should not bite *my sister,*" and later still to "*people* should not bite *sisters.*" When finally it knows that "*people* do not bite *people,*" the sequence is complete. Other processes may relate to toilet training, personal hygiene, or eating habits; such things will vary widely across cultures, though they are equally important in principle. Without the acquisition of the ability to generalize, socialization is incomplete and the child remains an "unsocialized being."

Here we may consider how, in a given group, community, village, tribe or nation, people become categorized as "deviant." Is it not related to the lack of fit between what they do and what the larger body approves of? Is it not a matter of their inability to generalize norms and to apply their knowledge systematically?[10] Then it should be easy for us to understand that what is seen as "normal" in one group might be judged "deviant" in another, and we are now brought back to the *social* construction of reality, or meaning, or virtue. We could be more subtle in approaching behavior and meaning if we distinguished the *generalization of norms* from the *generalization of others*: norms are generalized when one has moved from the specific to the general and from the individual to the totality (from "I must not steal this" to "stealing is not allowed"); the "other" is generalized when one moves from "Mommy" to "people" and from "is" to "ought." Thus a child develops a separation and a freedom from a specific parent or a specific "other" and is able to make generalizations appropriate to an ever widening (or more controlled) number of other people, generalizations which we ourselves would deem essential for Christians mature in the faith.

Failure to achieve generalization and internalization will produce serious problems for individuals and groups. In the west for example, the breakdown of both the extended and the nuclear family—due, among other things, to urban renewal, relocation, divorce and the biological revolution —has contributed to a high incidence of crime, especially among juveniles. Many youngsters exhibit a striking incompleteness of socialization; and the inability to internalize and generalize may in large part explain the incidence of recidivism. In such circumstances, is it appropriate to punish backsliding heavily? Where may Christian education and socialization encounter and assist such people, and what wisdom might missionaries glean from their own cultures?

In cultures until recently "traditional" in character, groups rather than isolated individuals may undertake the task of socializing their members. This, together with a greater permanence of extended families and a high fertility rate, has meant that children remain close to their "significant others" and to the sanctions wielded by the group. Thus is produced, at least in theory, a resilience of traditional processes of socialization and a tension between them and alternatives offered by outsiders. Inasmuch as formal education and literacy programs cut deep into traditional social processes, and inasmuch as these have been intrinsic to evangelization, Christian missionaries might well assess the effects of socialization on each generation and consider how western education is perceived locally. Without such an undertaking, grave misunderstandings will continue, and evangelization may never strike roots in certain cultures, or at certain times.

"Significant others" are those persons generally approved by the society as responsible for socializing someone. In the west we for long assumed that a father and a mother—married to each other, and biological parents of the child—were the crucial "significant others." But even in Victorian times the father was often less than a stable presence, and in our own day, quite apart from surrogate or foster parents, we have children reared by biological parents and then later by one biological parent and one stepparent, or those who live with one parent for most of the time and visit the other occasionally, or those who live with mother but experience a series of "friends" of mother, rather than a single, stable, "significant other" in the role of father. Such permutations demonstrate how widely "significant others" vary, and underline some of the practical problems associated with socialization and its component parts. But in the west or not, mission-minded Christians need to address questions like the following: Who are the stable "significant others" in the early life of the child? What influence do such people exert? What provisions are there for situations in which a "significant other" is not available? What happens if the process breaks down, not exceptionally but regularly? Are some cultures better adapted than others at dealing with socialization? Such questions we may acknowledge as important, precisely as we turn from them to more "practical" considerations; but they will not go away, and until they are frankly addressed, our mission programs will be built on sand.

Another issue concerns the identity that missionaries project among the people they purport to serve. How do we insert ourselves into the culture of others? Are we really assimilated and respected, or simply accommodated and tolerated? Does what we say and do become reinforced by the "significant others" in a society—the parents and elders? Or are we struggling upstream, only to find that we lose our hard-won gains, because whenever we are *not* present—in the villages or the houses or the classrooms, at recreation or in the fields—there takes place a "retraining" of the people by the *really* significant others in the society? Without some form of enduring legitimation—whereby what missionaries do is acknowledged to represent what the "elders" or the teachers approve of—missionaries are doomed to frustration, and the church will never be the kind of community that can perpetuate itself through time; there will always be the obsession by outsiders to educate every generation anew.

Part of socialization, though we cannot pursue it here, addresses the appropriation of sexual identity. This is intrinsic to the process of becoming human and social. Society—meaning not so much a dictator or one specific "significant other" but "the group," "the consensus," "the peers," "the elders" or "the sanction-holders" (and this will be problematic for missionaries persuaded of their own authority and importance)—dictates the meaning of sexual identity and clarifies the legitimate and illegitimate exercise of sexuality. To remain an active member of a social group, one must respect its sexual demands. And where fertility and generativity are intimately tied up with sexual responsibility, socialization must squarely address issues of sexuality. Therefore, certain questions should be asked of missionaries: What sexual identity do *we* project? What is *our* attitude to sexuality? Are *we* perceived as sexual beings? If we are professionally celibate, are we credible and understood?[11] How is social responsibility related to celibacy: are they not incompatible? Do we understand and respect the socialization processes which give meaning and dignity to the lives of others, or are we perceived to disapprove, or to be trying to change them?[12]

The kinds of questions that intrigue me are related not only to what missionaries *do,* but to how we are perceived. For if missionary intentions were not clear to people, is it any wonder that people did not respond as missionaries might have liked? And conversely, if today the local people are not understood by missionaries in the way they might hope for, is it surprising that behavior and motivations are misconstrued and impugned? A real knowledge of socialization, both in one's own life and in the lives of others, is necessary for self-understanding and for communication. And missionaries, more than most, are in that business!

PRIMARY SOCIALIZATION

We can now characterize primary socialization more precisely as that part of the process of becoming human and social that relates to the generalization of norms and others, to the point at which these are firmly embedded in one's consciousness. At this point, the child has created its first, enduring world.

We might be familiar with the term "the use of reason"; this is essentially the stage by which primary socialization is achieved, for it indicates the ability to generalize and to see oneself as a responsible agent. The child now knows the difference between right and wrong, we might say. But we must remember that "right and wrong" are something *each* society weighs and balances, and that their specific form may vary widely across cultures. Children who have completed primary socialization, therefore, are not uniform, but should be able to make responsible decisions about the particular world in which they live.

Language plays an immensely important mediating function in socialization, so much so that someone without language is virtually unsocializable. This is not to say that mutes cannot be responsible people; they indeed may have language, even though they lack speech. The "Wild Boy of Aveyron" stands as a type of the individual who is intractable until and unless tamed by language. And this now leads to a central issue for missionaries: how do *we* measure up, in respect of language? And intimately associated is the question whether we can ever, and in any sense, become socialized by the people and into the society where we minister? If we are not able to piece together an "enduring world" and if we do not understand the difference between right and wrong *as perceived within the society,* can we ever be trusted by the people, or must we remain peripheral and they uncommitted? I am certainly not arguing for a cosy relativism or forgetfulness of personal standards, but I question how we can call and challenge people unless we have some real experience of their experience, and how we can hope to make sense to them if they make no sense to us.

Missionaries rarely experience primary socialization in the community in which they minister. So how can we forge the links necessary for partnership? Language acquisition may help us construct reality somewhat as the native speakers do; it is a start. But it must go hand in hand with the integrated acquisition of culture. To learn languages bookishly is to avoid or overlook the kind of natural interaction intrinsic to the learning of language which takes place in primary socialization. Unless we find some way to engage in the socialization processes as they are experienced by our people, we will never make much sense, of them or to them. Their group and their socialization predated us; we must find a convergence, or evangelization will be marked by tragic divergence. This is a lifetime's agenda, and we will address it again in our final chapter.

SECONDARY SOCIALIZATION

If socialization generally is the process whereby rules and meaning are appropriated, created, and shared by peoples-in-groups, then clearly the group or groups to which an individual relates deserve some attention. And since people move in and out of groups throughout a lifetime, just as certain groups exercise greater or less control over individuals, the process whereby individuals relate to groups is also worthy of study if we are to understand the dynamics of socialization.

Assuming a person has negotiated the rapids of primary socialization and sailed on into a broad river of culture, fed by its streams and tributaries of meaning, the course is by no means complete. Just as rivers are characterized by flooding and spate, eddies and narrows, so change, reappraisal, rebellion, experimentation, and the testing of sanctions are only some of the hazards and challenges that mark our lives. A child who knows the difference between right and wrong *as laid down by significant others,* or one who responds to imperatives *when these are backed by sanctions,* will become the adult who will not always be dogged by those same significant others, not to mention the sanctions. What will be the response then?

"Secondary socialization" is the process—probably never-ending, and overlapping the concluding phases of primary socialization—whereby an individual transforms and applies the lessons of primary socialization, achieving a personal synthesis of behavior patterns, and a response to the existential realities of life. No longer is it adequate for one to apply rules based solely on the authority or persuasiveness of others; novel situations arise, extenuating circumstances occur, and self-interest modifies many responses. If an adult, ostensibly well launched on the open sea, returns to hug the coast, fearful of the water, or abandons all attempts at navigation, then such a one is judged unfree or immature; all the more reason therefore why people must experiment, vacillate, change, and build up experience on which they can draw as they encounter a range of unprecedented situations. During secondary socialization—typically adolescence and beyond—people discover imperatives and alternatives; where there are multiple alternatives there is diversity of response, and where there are no alternatives there is uniformity of response. Cultures manifest a wonderful range of forms of secondary socialization: age-grades, peer pressure, schools, seminaries, and many other rites of passage. All help to move the individual from child to adult.

If in ritual situations such as a formal sacrifice there should be uniformity of response on the part of the people, then either there are strong and efficient sanctions against deviance, or there is a very high degree of consensus among the participants. Or perhaps there are simply no perceived alternatives. And if—as at a dance or a festival—there appears to be an enormously varied response, then either there is a careful division of labor which allocates each person a specific task, or people feel that many courses of action are equally valid. But outsiders cannot legitimately judge, since they do not share the socialization common to the insiders; and the insiders should know—if they have been adequately trained—how to comport themselves. Only with careful detective work will an adequate interpretation by an outsider be possible. And inasmuch as we stand in unfamiliar situations, whether as "private individuals" or as Christian believers, we cannot and must not assume that we understand the nature or the motivations of the behavior, much less that we can stand on the edges of other cultures and judge or condemn. Socialization processes serve the interests of the group; they do not have to make intuitive sense to outsiders, any more than does language or a Tridentine mass, the stock exchange or a cricket match.

Assuming that a society, as we have characterized it, does not treat them as criminal or deviant, then those who are acknowledged as "serious" or "mature" or "orthodox" (that is, those who adequately exemplify the fully socialized person) are normally themselves legitimated as judges of what is acceptable, good, moral, honorable or noble. Outsiders have little of relevance to say to the insider, unless they become assimilated, legitimated: in a word, socialized. Hence the importance not only of missionaries approaching other cultures with respect and finesse, but of Christians rejoicing to discover that communities already incarnate gospel values, rather than trying to "convert" such communities to behavior and belief that are quite unrealistic and morally impossible.

Understanding of secondary socialization will teach us that, in becoming mature social animals, people *must* use the elements of culture—relationships, rules, sanctions—that already exist, and *must* synthesize these into a personalized, coherent and socially acceptable whole. Thus the Christian and missionary would have to admit that the unfamiliar "grace builds on culture" is as axiomatic as "grace builds on nature." Both nature and culture may need to be challenged and perfected; neither should be overlooked, demeaned, or destroyed.

Secondary socialization is about rearranging and rebuilding, as a person learns to live responsibly and socially, in a real world, blending self-interest with civic duty. But there are many different kinds of social groups and many different but acceptable ways of being an individual and a citizen; so it should not surprise us that there is more than one pattern of secondary socialization. And just as socialization varies across societies and different social groups "select out" for different qualities, so there will be many different responses to the gospel. Inasmuch as we understand the processes of socialization at work—whether among indigenous populations, Christians, or missionaries of different times and cultures, denominations and theological traditions—so we should be able to predict and interpret some of the responses to evangelization. For it is not simply about "the gospel" as it impinges on "culture" but about values and traditions and morality, about real people of flesh and blood living in a specific situation; evangelization must be sensitive to these realities.

Could we ever think that "the gospel," as mediated by Swiss Calvinist missionaries of the 1880s to, say, a highly centralized kingdom in Muslim Cameroons, would have been preached or perceived in anything like the same way as "the gospel" as mediated by Irish Roman Catholic missionaries of the 1950s to, say, the heavily "Christianized" Igbo people of Nigeria? Then is there any justification for missionaries to assume that either "the gospel" or "culture" is so uniform as to imply or warrant a universal policy for the evangelization of cultures? And lest we cry that Christians have never naively espoused a uniform approach either to "the gospel" or to "culture," perhaps we should scrutinize the history of our attitudes both to theology and to anthropology. We have tended to treat them as if they were monolithic, unitary and unchanging, in spite of the undoubted fact, muffled more often than trumpeted, that there have been denominational and historical variations in theology, and that a Zulu is rather different from a Zande.

Tacitly at least, we have tended to treat people of other cultures as uniform, when real virtue would have admitted that a pastoral plan for one area might be quite inappropriate for another. But often Christians in mission have perpetuated pastoral plans which either exist in a state of inertia, or were imported—stamped "success"—from another time and place. If we paid very close attention to the patterns of socialization as they operate in different cultures and at different times (not forgetting our own), then perhaps we would be able to formulate even more dynamic and relevant pastoral approaches which embody respect for the uniqueness of individuals and cultures and allow for a real inculturation—an authentic indigenization, translation, and incarnation—of the living word of God across time and space, a word already spoken "at various times in the past, and in various different ways, [and] in our own time" (Heb 1:1-2).

SOCIALIZATION AND SCHOOLING

Many missionaries of earlier times recognized the force of socialization processes, at least implicitly, since they frequently confessed their inability to achieve much, once the people had reached adulthood. However, instead of using the indigenous processes in order to facilitate a mature response to the Christian message, some missionaries in effect abandoned the adults, railed at the imperviousness of the people to Christian truth, and turned their attention to the children. Typically, though not universally, they found little to respect in local society and mores; far less did they own that God was there before them; all of which merely illustrates the strength of their own selective socialization!

Some missionaries implicitly but naively espoused the classical Jesuit philosophy, assuming that, given access to the youngsters, they would be able to retain their allegiance throughout life; perhaps they thought that such children were "tabulae rasae" and entirely suggestible to the processes of the classroom. If so they were sadly deceived.[13] Far from being uneducated, the children were simply not schooled in formal western ways; but whatever they learned in the classroom had to be legitimated or expunged by their parents. Certainly, some of what the missionaries taught, stuck. Equally certainly, much was as if blown away on the evening breeze. The missionaries might well have had the children in their custodial care for a few hours a day; but the real "significant others" came into their own once school was over, and the processes of re-education and socialization continued. Very little of any consequence, if not legitimated by the chiefs and elders, was allowed to strike roots and flourish unchecked in the lives of the children.

Missionaries who thought that western-style education would solve the problem of making Christians were of course wrong; not all were that simple. But many did fail to notice or comprehend that as fast as they educated the infants, the adolescents were leaving school. And if the former seemed obedient and malleable, the latter were independent and volatile. The promise of the classroom seemed to evaporate once the doors were opened and the pupils left school. Likewise, if adults felt themselves over-looked by missionaries in favor of the children, then they began to identify missionary Christianity itself with their children and not with themselves. So Christianity came to be seen as rather harmless and perhaps even good for children, but something they would grow out of once they became mature and reflective! Certainly, when they left school and became mar-riageable—more specifically, sexually active—most seemed an embarrass-ment to the missionaries, and ceased to be communicants until they were widowed or dying, and thus deemed to be sexually inactive. Missionaries might occupy the trenches of primary socialization, but local adults and "significant others" occupied almost all of the high ground.

Socialization, then, is not confined to the classroom or to formal educa-tion; it is a continuous process most commonly happening informally, in "practical training" and through social bonding and sharing. The very schooling seen by missionaries as indispensable appeared insignificant or irrelevant to the perceived priorities of people in oral rather than literate cultures. And because it used a foreign language, such education would never be assimilated like the values held dear by the people.[14]

The question of evangelization and literacy, or of literacy and modern-ization, is extremely pertinent and will be dealt with more systematically later. But we note here that no matter how inspired the "good news," without adequate "translation" enormous confusion will ensue. Evangeli-zation absolutely must intersect with indigenous socialization; it does not depend on formal schooling. And evangelization absolutely must focus on the adults, the first and most significant educators of the children; unless adults are approached with respect and in dialogue, they will not be moti-vated to evangelize the children, and the latter will not assimilate the faith. And if children have only a veneer of Christianity they will never be inclined later on to pass the tradition to their own children. So, the only certainty is that missionaries will have made themselves alien to the people and yet indispensable for evangelization; there will be no mature community of believers, and each generation will be receiving different messages from the missionaries and from their "significant others."

If it works through local processes of socialization, and if it directly addresses the adults, then evangelization absolutely must operate through the language of the people. In a "foreign" or a second language, it can never be assimilated as an indigenous experience. And without indigenization, the "good news" will not spread like wildfire. Christians will be forced to demean or repudiate their own family or community. And while occasionally someone might legitimately respond to Christianity in defiance of the community, this cannot be the normal response, since evangelization should be directed at the individual-in-community, and lead to the renewal of the whole group rather than its fragmentation.

SOCIALIZATION AND THE ACQUISITION OF KNOWLEDGE

Socialization is no more to be equated with the simple acquisition of knowledge than is formal education; to think so is to miss an important point about privileged knowledge, and about knowledge as a scarce resource. Socialization is as much about learning to discriminate between various kinds of knowledge and knowledge-brokers, and not intruding into restricted areas, as it is about amassing interesting or useful knowledge. Similarly, formal education should not be about being taught all the specific pieces of knowledge needed throughout life. Both socialization and formal education should be "generative" (we have looked at "generalization") if they are to be successful: that is, they should provide rules and an interpretative style, a "habitus" or moral sense, which, applied to new situations, will enable one to produce an appropriate and worthy response.

A rule of thumb for missionaries might be this: flexibility and adaptability, and not a fixed or predetermined approach. Yet who can implement such plans if an elaborate missionary bureaucracy is already in place? But what are the alternatives? If Christians and missionaries attempt to isolate people in order to indoctrinate them, they will inevitably fail to produce Christian communities. If Christian education is focused primarily on the formal situation of the classroom, it will never equip people for their real life-experience. If educators and missionaries do not allow for a "generative" component in people's responses, behavior will be mechanical and true inculturation will never take place. If adults do not respect classroom education or if they judge it merely for children, they will never respect a Christianity that is rooted in the classroom. And if people's own institutions of socialization and knowledge-mongering are not respected by Christians and missionaries, they will simply not respond.

Exceptionally, however, where there is very rapid social change, people may be bemused by any novelty, and traditional lines of authority and sanction will be under severe strain. But where the traditionalism is strong, people will conform to conservative patterns of behavior; and unless missionaries are seen to respect these, they will ultimately be deemed irrelevant. Commonly today, people live in social environments which are neither completely "traditional" nor entirely "open" to outside influence: traditional authority may be under some threat but western novelty is viewed with suspicion or ambivalence. In such circumstances we might expect that the local response to evangelization will be unsystematic and confused, and so unless missionaries are extremely responsive to local sensibilities, the result might well be the proliferation of dual religious systems or syncretism.[15]

All societies "institutionalize" knowledge; it can be propagated, but also restricted. Certain people—bone-setters, medicine-men, diviners or priests—will jealously guard their knowledge; and some social institutions, such as the so-called "secret societies," will prosper precisely because of their ability to remain exclusive. To be an adult is to have access to some forms of knowledge, to be excluded from others, and to know the "rules of the game."[16] How is a potential Christian to respond to a Christianity that is unclear or misunderstood on the subject of esoteric and exoteric knowledge? Is it really all to be found in the classroom, or is some held by the priests? Are local people really invited to become priests or deacons, ministers or chairpersons, or are the qualifications effectively so unrealistic as to perpetuate the exclusiveness of the expatriate priesthood and maintain the ultimate authority of the missionary? If a local community is the church, why is it so dependent on outsiders for finance, for personnel, and for orthodoxy? Does Christianity acknowledge the pressures of the real world in which people live, or is it addressed only to a world beyond? How are people to be persuaded that the community of believers really does bleed or rejoice in the existential situation, if the people's socialization processes and wisdom are not assimilated and woven into the seamless garment of the church?

Incarnating the Gospel

A thorough, rather than a well-meaning and general, understanding of processes of socialization as they impinge on real people in real situations seems to be mandatory if there is to be authentic incarnation of the gospel across cultures. And unless that understanding modifies the ways in which we evangelize, *and* our responses to the people, it is difficult to see us doing anything other than imposing and enforcing our "package" on others. Even given our unquestioned good intentions, we simply must not create situations which leave it morally impossible for people to respond to our invitation; either the invitation needs rephrasing or we must withdraw. It is intolerable for us to assume that because evangelization—as we understand it, and from our own socio-religious context—makes sense and is legitimate (and even obligatory!), we are thereby justified in proceeding to another community on our own terms, disrupting it with the "dangerous knowledge" of the gospel, and then leaving the onus entirely on the people.[17]

To fail to respect and respond to socialization processes in other cultures is tantamount to saying one or other of the following:

1. *There is no significant difference between a Zulu and an American; a Bantu and a Briton are much the same.*

However universalistic and tolerant this judgment may seem, its true colors are revealed if, instead of imagining that a Zulu can pass easily as an American, or a Bantu as a Briton, we imagine ourselves—American, Briton or whatever—deposited in South Africa or Zaire, lacking any knowledge of the local language, isolated and confused. Then it becomes clear just how monumental are the differences between oneself and another. And it becomes palpably obvious that one person's socialization processes are of extremely limited applicability or appropriateness in an unfamiliar situation.

2. *There is only one way to approach other people, for evangelization or anything else, and that is mine.*

Clearly this is a much cruder approach, and more easily unmasked. Yet missionaries seem to have forgotten it many times, in their haste, or zeal, or insecurity. But however we may sympathize with one who adopts a certain posture, assuming it to be always and uniquely valid, we must declare unequivocally that this is inappropriate, in fact indefensible for a missionary. Anyone who undertakes, by leaving home and culture, to implement the centrifugal imperative of Christianity must nevertheless learn to treat the other as subject and not as object. This means *listening* to and *receiving* from the other the matrix or blueprint through which he or she understands the world. *That* is the existential reality. *That* is the point from which other people are called to respond to the gospel. To overlook or repudiate this is to depart from the way of Jesus, who came to seek and to find people and to address them in the context of their own lives. Only if we meet people on their turf—epistemological as well as geographical—can we communicate. The burden is on ourselves, not initially on them, to be respectful, comprehensible, and relevant.

3. *"The Gospel" Is More Important Than People*

This is indeed a problem for some; "woe to me if I do not preach the gospel," we may say. Or we may think that if we do "preach the gospel" (as if it were as simple as that!), then people should "take it or leave it"; if the latter, they are in bad faith. But Jesus came to bring an abundance of life, and never failed to address persons, emphasizing the priority of people over things, laws, and even the sabbath. It is not legitimate (as already noted) for us to foist our interpretation of the gospel on people without reference to the realities of their lives. Nor may we pass judgment on those who do not respond to our expectations, especially if we hardly understand their own perceptions and interpretations of what we have to say. A law which cannot be obeyed loses its moral force. Have we missionaries failed to notice the moral impossibility of what we demanded? And have we taken steps to improve the situation? Sometimes, yes; but threats and sanctions may be inappropriate and unjust; and unless missionaries understand the social and moral conditions underpinning the lives of the communities in which we minister, we will not be able to facilitate life-giving change in collaboration with local communities. And, of course, without such change and collaboration, "the gospel" will become an oppressive load (see Lk 11:46) that we try to impose, rather than a liberating word of life and love.

It is a sobering thought that if the gospel had been more effectively inculturated—offered to and accepted by societies—then the church in many parts of the world would look very different, and many contemporary missionaries would be free to be challenged by situations of first evangelization—preaching the gospel where it has never been preached— rather than tied to routine jobs in local churches dependent on expatriates for more than a century. Collaboration is much to be applauded; dependency that prevents self-reliance is a sin and a shame. Another sobering thought: it is widely true that not only has the senior generation not taken responsibility for educating the junior generation in the faith, but the wisdom and integrity of parents and grandparents has been a resource often overlooked or wasted by Christian churches as they preached a gospel of love and respect.

And so we return to our initial questions about the possibility of bonding with other people, and about the human capacity for creative change and adaptation. And it has to be said that people cannot easily move across cultures; the human species is relatively culture-bound, especially once language and socialization have been imparted and assimilated. Most people do not cross the boundaries of their own culture, at least not freely and for long. Many of our points of reference, notably our language and habits, do not travel well. Most people instinctively resist becoming strangers in another social world, or else group into ghettos with others of familiar language or habits, the better to maintain their identity and integrity. Most people behave in these ways. But missionaries are different, and herein lies a rich paradox.

Missionaries deliberately undertake to cross cultural and linguistic boundaries, a monumental undertaking not only redolent of excitement but fraught with confusion. In the ensuing interaction, much will depend on missionaries' expectations and finesse, dispositions that require careful training.

If we who set sail for other cultures and worlds assume that we will ultimately be able to—or indeed that we should—understand the local people comprehensively, then we are not so much simple as arrogant; how would we feel if a "foreigner" presumed to behave in our presence like one of "us," with all our native casualness? And if we do recognize our differences from the outset and yet assume that all and only our own points of reference will continue to be valid, then we are tainted with imperialism, bigotry or totalitarianism, certainly not with the Spirit of Christ. No, we have to do considerably better than that, and at the same time discover ways of engaging in the mutual liberation and enlightenment of all humanity.

If we Christians really examine how we came to be who we are, we shall have uncovered our formative socialization processes. Then we will understand how easily things might have been otherwise! Reflecting carefully, we will draw lessons from our own openness to or our fear of strangers. We will be able to own our conservatism or radicality, our certainties and doubts, and some of the fears to which we are heir; and we will be sensitive to the enormous range of social processes—normal or pathological, by our own or anyone else's standards—that have made other people similar or different. But we will not forget that people are different as well as similar, unique as well as comparable. And we will never seek "lowest common denominator" solutions, where human beings are involved.

We missionaries, imbued with the Spirit of Jesus, will pray to be delivered from the temptation to assume crudely that our own synthesis and world view, our own responses and initiatives, are the only possible or valid ones. We will strive to respect the integrity of others and the reality of other cultures and other experiences, and we will honestly try to understand and appreciate the processes of socialization that have made other people who and what they are. Finally, we will painfully learn that we, and not only others, are odd, unpredictable, sometimes secretive, ambivalent and occasionally unreliable; and we will pray to rejoice in these confusing realities, as we undertake the pilgrimage which leads us away from the babel and toward the vernacular—the local ways, the indigenous language, the new world of meaning, and the honest hearts of the people—where the reign of God can surely be found to flourish.

Notes and Bibliography

1. Still a classic is the book by L.C. Dunn and T. Dobzhansky, *Heredity, Race, and Society,* New York, Mentor Books, 1946. The entry under "Race," in the *Encyclopedia of the Social Sciences,* by Marvin Harris, is comprehensive. Dictionary definitions of "race," however, can sometimes confuse. I am not competent to write about genetics, but refer here only to race and culture and their essential *separability* from genetic considerations.

2. From *The Wild Boy of Aveyron,* by Harlan Lane, London, Paladin Books, 1979. This is a fascinating account of studies done with and on an adolescent boy. It places us in the context of eighteenth and nineteenth century thought, and describes well the struggle toward a definition of "human" which had exercised theologians and humanists for years.

3. From R.C. Lewontin; quoted in *The Flamingo's Smile: Reflections in Natural History,* by Stephen Jay Gould, New York, Norton Publishers, 1985.

4. Again, Jay Gould, *loc. cit.* This is one of the author's exciting popularizations of biology and paleontology; the essay considers the contingency of

human equality, and is well worth pondering from a theological and pastoral, if a somewhat theoretical, perspective.

5. Jack Dominian's insights in the field of counseling and psychiatry are born of a deep personal faith in Jesus, and are always helpful and sometimes very striking. On the question of human flexibility he is particularly relevant for those working for change in cultures other than their own. See particularly *Cycles of Affirmation,* London, Darton, Longman and Todd, 1975.

6. Helpful, accessible, and clearly presented works on the subject of how different people see the world include *The Cultural Context of Learning and Thinking,* by M. Cole, J. Glick, J. Gay and D.W. Sharp, New York, Basic Books, 1971, and, more recently, *The Psychology of Literacy,* Cambridge, Mass., Harvard University Press, 1981, by M. Cole and S. Scribner. This latter has some interesting things to say about language, a topic we will consider in the next chapter.

7. This example comes from Evans-Pritchard's work, *Nuer Religion,* Oxford, Blackwells, 1956:84. It is quoted by Mary Douglas in a section—and a book—which is of profound relevance to missionaries: see *Purity and Danger,* Harmondsworth, UK, Penguin Books 1966:39.

8. For fascinating information about the way people "see" and interpret their world, the person to consult is the great Russian psychologist A.R. Luria. See particularly *Cognitive Development: Its Cultural and Social Foundations,* edited by M. Cole, Cambridge, Mass., Harvard University Press, 1976.

9. More than twenty years old, and still green, is *The Social Construction of Reality,* by Peter Berger and Thomas Luckmann, New York, Doubleday, 1966. They trace the paths by which a person becomes a member of a social group, showing how "free choice" is subject to social constraints and sanctioned by authority-figures. I have found this invaluable, if difficult at times; and in the present section I rely heavily on these authors.

10. *The Human Cycle,* by Colin Turnbull, New York, Simon and Schuster, 1983, takes as its theme the process of growing up, maturing, and aging. But instead of looking at these things purely in terms of "other cultures," Turnbull draws on his own experiences, showing how similar and how different they are, to some of the other experiences he charts. It is a humorous and insight-filled account of "normalness" and "deviancy."

11. Donald Goergen's book, *The Sexual Celibate,* New York, Seabury, 1974, tackles a number of problematic but always relevant issues in the field of celibacy and sexuality. Contemporary cross-cultural evangelization, as well as ministry of and to people from western societies, is highlighting some of the implications of celibacy. The "public image" of celibacy needs much clarification in these days, and Goergen's book contributes to the debate.

12. Clifford Geertz has a particularly lively essay about sexual identity and shows how limited is much of our thinking. He examines different societies'

attitudes to sexual variation, and there is a wealth of challenging thoughts for Christians. See *Local Knowledge*, New York, Basic Books, Harper/Colophon, 1983, Chapter 4, "Common Sense as a Cultural System": 73–93. For a necessary female perspective on many issues connected with sexuality or socialization, there is a book of essays and papers covering many cultures, edited by Michelle Z. Rosaldo and Louise Lamphere, *Woman, Culture, and Society*, California, Stanford University Press, 1974.

13. Ivan Illich is perhaps the best known critic of uncritical literacy programs; his writings are voluminous. Anyone unfamiliar with his style cannot fail to be caught up in his passion about some of what he considers to be egregious errors of missionaries. Helpful in the present context are, certainly, *Deschooling Society*, New York, Harper and Row, 1970, and Chapters 8 and 9 of *Celebration of Awareness*, New York, Doubleday, 1969.

14. A rather scholarly and informative volume, *Culture Theory*, edited by R. Shweder and R. LeVine, Cambridge, Cambridge University Press, 1984, contains one of Clifford Geertz' acclaimed essays, "From the Native's Point of View" (Chapter 4). Also, Chapter 10, "The Development of Competence in Culturally Defined Domains," is interesting, as indeed are many other sections of this book.

15. We have already noted Robert Schreiter's *Constructing Local Theologies*, New York, Orbis Books, 1985; London, SCM 1985. Missionaries should know this book, I feel. Schreiter deals at some length with syncretism and dual religious systems in Chapter 7:144–158.

16. It is important that we be aware of the sexual division of knowledge, as well as the sexual differentiation of socialization. Missionaries may stand accused—as indeed are most educators—of not paying adequate attention to the specific learning modes of girls and women, and thus of harming their psychosocial development. Many worthy books are now available, but one which has most caught the imagination is *In a Different Voice: Psychological Theory and Women's Development*, by Carol Gilligan, Cambridge, Mass., Harvard University Press, 1982. Also, there is a useful section in Walter Ong's *Fighting for Life: Contest, Sexuality, and Consciousness*, Ithaca, NY, Cornell University Press, 1981:64ff; 113f.

17. Again, see Vincent Donovan's *Christianity Rediscovered: An Epistle from the Masai*, originally published by Notre Dame, Indiana, Fides/Claretian Press, 1978, and in New York by Orbis Books, 1982, then London, SCM Press 1982. Fifth impression 1987. Donovan follows up the implications of real sensitivity to people of other cultures; if you offer something freely, it is important to be open to the possibility of people's gently declining your offering. Missionaries have probably not considered this seriously enough, yet it must be at the heart of any relationship. We deal with this in greater detail in Chapter Four, where we talk about gifts.

Three

Language, Thinking, and Evangelization

Does language help us contact and name reality, or does it imprison us and reinforce prejudice? How does language confer and control power? What use is literacy? Can missionaries ever really understand local people? If not, how can we ever respect them?

Missionaries and Language

Historically, as we know, missionaries have been agents of change as they met people with unfamiliar tongues, brought their own languages to the interaction, and always sought to communicate through reciprocity. For just as the transmission of special messages is central to a missionary's sense of vocation, so also is simple interpersonal exchange and mutual enrichment. Missionaries have been responsible for some of the finest scholarship in language studies, from philology to semantics, from grammatology to comparative linguistics, from the creation of new scripts to the phonetic notation of unwritten languages. And there is a proud heritage here, which bears fruit in our day and across the world. The study and practice of language has been and is intrinsic to mission.

Today, few topics are more likely to provoke missionaries to passionate discussion and argument, than language; every missionary has something to say, some deep-seated belief or attitude to impart, some justification or explanation to invoke, some position to defend, some co-missionary to judge, when the issue arises. Nerves may scream and tempers rise, but rarely are people dispassionate when they talk about language in mission.

Missionaries both reflect and help to create ways of thinking, philosophies, and theologies; and because all these things change over time, it is unsurprising that missionary attitudes have varied widely, and continue to do so. Since language is a vehicle—with an effective monopoly on transportation—and human thinking is its passenger, we might expect that attitudes to the one will affect attitudes to the other; and so it proves. Sometimes the striking uniqueness of an untranslatable word or phrase leads to borrowing, and it becomes incorporated into our language, and hallowed: "pyjamas," "poltergeist," "blitz," "at death's door," "pussy-willow." At other times our own language fails before the unknown or never-before-experienced sights or sounds of another culture, and at best we can only use an indigenous term that does not travel well into our own linguistic context: *halei, nganga, kula, potlatch.* We can always *try* to maintain communication across the chasms formed by abutting languages. But sometimes we fail to do so, from tiredness or frustration or incapacity; or we tolerate communication only along a single, narrow, fragile, one-way linguistic suspension bridge—in our own familiar tongue or according to our own interpretations—forgetting that communication should move simultaneously in two directions, creating constantly tested chains of reciprocity between all parties, if it is to facilitate rather than to obscure understanding.

Our thoughts turn, in the present chapter, to some of the perspectives that have inspired, accompanied, and perhaps undermined missionary endeavor. And we will try to keep in binocular focus both the message and the messengers: the word of God and those who bring good news of peace.

Looking and Seeing

REALITY AND RELEVANCE

We noted, when considering socialization, that very often different people notice different things and draw different conclusions when faced with the same objective reality. This can be striking enough when the people share a common culture; where there are wide cultural divergences the differences can be almost total, having very serious repercussions. Quite apart from observational acuity, there is another—and, for us, profoundly important —reason for selective perception: relevance.

It is difficult to overemphasize the significance of relevance, both to the way we behave and indeed to the kind of people we are. In early socialization we learn what others see as relevant and important for a well-behaved person; from the earliest phases of secondary socialization, we are selecting and rejecting from a myriad of possibilities, as we refashion a world according to our developing priorities and sense of relevance. Relevance— whether in a very concrete sense (writing this book is relevant to me now), or whether in a more principled, philosophical sense (I believe prayer is relevant to my personal wholeness)—is at the core of our lives. And of course the opposite is also true; those who find it difficult to choose what is relevant for them, or who are constantly changing, or who cannot find anything satisfactorily or enduringly relevant, will live in a world without a hub, shorn of meaning and lacking focus.

As we look across cultures we can hardly fail to be struck by the way in which relevance is culturally determined. People in one culture are as sure of the relevance of certain things they do as are people in other cultures when they behave quite differently; and each will be able to justify a way of action that the other may find bizarre or even offensive. A simple example is the sounds of languages: some of the sounds relevant to a Xhosa or Tamil speaker are similar to, and some different from, those relevant to an English speaker; within the appropriate community, Korean phonology is entirely relevant, and certainly does not sound odd. And if a Vietnamese person settles in the U.S. after learning Vietnamese, he or she will always retain some of the sound patterns and articulations of Vietnamese even while striving for approximations in English, since the individual assimilated a set of relevant sounds which cannot be entirely repudiated, even when separated from the legitimating community. Or consider matters of religious relevance: in cultures in which religion—attitudes, belief, rituals, sanctions —is "embedded" in the social fabric rather than institutionalized as a discrete entity—with its times and places of service and worship, its separating rather than its uniting functions, and its dogmatism and codifications—one can see greater homogeneity of religion-and-culture, less variation in people's responses and behavior, and a much greater consensus as to what really is relevant in life.

We missionaries are usually very clear about what is relevant, both to ourselves and to others, for we believe that we bear a message which is really good news for all times and cultures. But we are not exactly "typical" members of our own cultural groups, and we are in fact counter-cultural inasmuch as we espouse causes and ways of life that are not reflected in the cultural mainstream. Nevertheless we take pride in our sense of purpose and we wish to share it. But people in other cultures are not empty slates, and they inhabit a world of which we know little: an enduring world, and a world which encodes its own relevance. Leaving aside for a moment the question of social change, individual alienation, the decline of moral values, revolution, colonialism and the rest, we should be able to grant that people feel "at home" in their own culture as much as we might feel at home in ours, that it is difficult for one person to feel emotionally and intellectually comfortable in another culture, and that a person's—or a people's—sense of what is relevant cannot easily or meaningfully be changed from outside, once it has become settled through processes of socialization. In other words, relevance is something inseparable from one's culture itself. And since culture is mediated essentially and primarily through language, we will have to examine language and linguistic processes if we are to begin to understand how people determine and adhere to what is relevant.

Let it be emphasized then: unless we who come as missionaries to another culture learn to recognize and respect other people's values (relevance), we will fail both to demonstrate the coherence and attractiveness of our own (since we will fail to bridge our respective worlds), and to present a living word for translation and assimilation. We may colonize people; we may get them to pass our examinations; we may present them with an alien—and irrelevant—moral system; but we will not bring into their world and families and lives such an extension of the reign of God as will be humanizing and liberating, and above all relevant.

INCLUSION AND EXCLUSION

There is a danger, particularly in western thinking, that we hold truths or hypotheses until they appear to be disproved, and then we abandon them for their opposites. We operate in terms of binary oppositions and we love to invoke the either/or dichotomy: a thing is either good or bad; people are either male or female; statements are either true or false, and so on. Even though a little reflection reminds us that life is rarely so simple, we cling to our way of thinking unless forced to make exceptions. But the wisdom of the east is much less absolute, more embracing: both/and is as helpful and valid as either/or. Perhaps we missionaries who come from a western tradition of propositional truth and codified dogma need to learn to approach knowledge with a both/and attitude; not only might it illuminate many areas of knowledge and experience, but it will certainly provide us with a key to the knowledge held in other cultures that do not canonize propositions, do not glorify codification, and do not need literacy to support their knowledge-system.

Consider the following question (which seems to seek a yes/no, either/or, answer): "Is Chicago far from Milwaukee, or London from Cambridge?" Depending on whether one is in a speedy vehicle or on foot, in a life-or-death race or with limitless time, the answer will vary; there is no single "right" answer. And depending on context, we might answer both "yes" and "no," as well as "not yes" or "not no." If we exclude any set of responses from our consideration, we have, as it were, arranged the world to suit ourselves; some languages and people would approach the question with a very open framework, both linguistic and interpretative.

A both/and approach to knowledge and relevance across cultures might be surprisingly helpful and freeing. Where possible we might try not to choose one pole and repudiate another, but consider how an inclusive (both/and) approach to knowledge might be helpful for the mutual communication we champion as missionaries. And we might inquire if such an attitude could more readily evoke indigenous responses to the word, responses which would indicate that the gospel was being authentically inculturated, becoming assimilated with integrity and relevance by the local church. A both/and approach would be open to the richness of the experience and the validity of the knowledge found in other cultures, and thus other people would be able to discover for themselves the relevance of Jesus and the gospel, just as the Jews and the pagans of Jesus' time were called to the same discovery.

Given our intended openness, we should be prepared for some surprises; and indeed we will discover a range of questions that may be both unexpected and crucial to our missionary approach.

THE SAPIR-WHORF PROBLEM

Does language shape thought? Is thinking enslaved by the language in which it takes place? Is an answer to be found with an either/or approach? Edward Sapir (1884–1939) and Benjamin Lee Whorf (1897–1941) put the linguistic cat well and truly among the cognitive pigeons! Both were fascinated by the way in which language shapes our cultural experience, and Whorf suggested that thought is virtually determined by language: we can only think what our language allows us to think. Now Whorf was no fool, and was familiar with the structure and function of some native American languages, to the point where he understood the limits of translation and translatability in ordinary life. And his area of study obviously underlines crucial questions for us. Can our ways of thinking ever change in a qualitative way? If not, what about other people's ways of thinking? What happens when we try to see things—interpret, assess, or think things—as another person from another culture and with another language does? And assuming we become aware of the difficulties we ourselves would face in trying to encode and decode our thinking in another speech and another place, what happens when other people try to make sense of our culturally and linguistically determined thinking, logic, meaning—and, of course, relevance? These are enormously important issues, for ourselves personally, and in relation to evangelization; and they bear serious consideration as we try to address questions such as: What changes do we expect in people who accept Christianity? Are our expectations realistic or fulfilled? Or, again, what kind of response is necessary and sufficient (indeed what is possible) from someone who hears the gospel encoded in an unfamiliar language and clothed in a foreign culture?

Neither Sapir nor Whorf actually formalized a hypothesis or systematic list of propositions concerning the relationship between language and thought; but extrapolating from their writings, we are asked to consider that:

(i) All higher levels of thinking are dependent on language.
(ii) The structure of one's native language influences the way in which one understands the environment. Thus the picture of the universe shifts from language to language.
(iii) Differences in the way in which people comprehend or find relevance in the world, are *causally* related to the structure of their language.[1]

Three points to make here: these are serious propositions; they merit consideration, not only from an either/or perspective, but insofar as they might be partially true or helpful; and let us not confuse "language" with "literacy," or even "verbal skill."

Identifying and Labeling

FROM CHAOS TO COSMOS

The world can be a frightening place. Even after we have spent many years becoming accustomed to some of its many facets and learning to pass from reaction to action, our control is very limited and our ease is very fragile.

We may know how it feels to be transported to a place where nobody speaks our language, where we sense our aloneness and ignorance, our incomprehension and lack of control; it is at best tedious, at worst quite fearsome. Many of our previous points of reference and points of view are no longer valid or shared; much of our wisdom and experience now counts for nothing; most of our frustrations cannot even be adequately conveyed to others.

Within our own group, and by the use of our own language, we can, fairly effectively, tame our environment and make friends with other people. And this we sedulously undertake—often quite un-self-consciously— as we become increasingly proficient and efficient members of our cultural and linguistic group. It is only when we are separated from our comfortable world that the true degree of our reliance on the shared conventions of language begins to be felt. And then perhaps we might realize the importance of the creative—or the "world-maintaining"—functions of our native tongue: the fact that it helps create and maintain a predictable and controllable world, and turn the threat of confusion or chaos into the potential of an enduring cosmos. Not surprisingly, therefore, language tends to be rather conservative; we like to be able to say what we mean, mean what we say, and articulate our view of reality and our ideas of relevance, without undue ambiguity or singularity.

And, likewise, let us not forget, every group with a shared language— and depending on exactly how these are calculated there are, conservatively, five thousand or so—is steadfastly building and maintaining its own world of meaning, and where necessary or advisable, resisting or repudiating others' ideas of reality, truth, beauty . . . and relevance.

NAMING AND POWER

In the book of Genesis we read of Adam giving names to everything in the world (Gen 2:20). Whoever can name things possesses a certain kind of power. Imagine that you know the name, in Greek or Armenian, Gaelic or Cornish, for "tree" or "mother" or "sky" or "God." And imagine being in a position of really wanting that knowledge, but of not having it! Clearly, the ability to name is the possession of power. If I give you my name, I give you power to name me; if I do not give you my name, you are ignorant—or, we might say, not "entitled" to it—and we remain strangers. The person who legitimately says "I name this ship 'Titanic,'" or "I baptize you in the name of the Trinity," or "I declare this bazaar open," is using words "performatively," really bringing about what the words say, and actually manifesting power. If I say "I give you my word," "I call upon these persons to witness," "I swear . . . so help me God," then I am engaged in a communicative act which binds me into a community and in a significant sense changes the world. I am reconstructing the order of things. I am acting with power.[2]

If language is power, then its lack is powerlessness, and this remains true whether we recognize it or not. I, personally, am powerless in Arabic and Russian. Perhaps I feel that I can manage well enough without them; but if ever they are the means of communication where I am, I shall be almost entirely excluded—until and unless I am empowered. But if I feel that I absolutely need them, then I will want to become . . . literate. Anyone who aspires to some form of social and cultural (and thus linguistic) power, however modest, will, in the modern world, need to acquire literacy: the ability to manipulate the formal system of a language, through reading and writing, as well as through speaking. And anyone who wishes, for whatever reason, to empower others to drink at the pool of knowledge encoded in a particular culture (and therefore language) will concentrate very heavily on affording access to literacy skills.

Possession of language is now so widely deemed to be synonymous with literacy that if people do not have literacy they tend to be described—pejoratively—as illiterate: that is, lacking something. But in our rush to offer literacy to others, we have often failed to notice and respect the genius of the people and of their own language. For the opposite of literacy is *not* illiteracy—except in an either/or mentality, and according to a certain kind of etymological logic; the alternative to literacy—that is, the way in which knowledge is encoded, stored, circulated and transmitted—is orality. Literacy is to letters and scripts and texts as orality is to speech and discourse and conversation. Literacy is as good a method of storing formal knowledge, propositional truths, fossilized facts, as orality is of nurturing informal knowledge, wisdom, and living truth. Literacy can be a fine museum; but orality is a better laboratory.

If the purpose of evangelization is to transmit legal briefs, eternal truths, absolute injunctions and systematic and comprehensive catechisms, then literacy is probably as necessary to evangelization as is baptism. But if evangelization is more about communication between living people, about the uttering of a living word, about the incarnation of the word in culture, and about an urgent and vibrant call to action, then orality certainly needs to be re-examined as a possible vehicle. And even if we remain unconvinced that literacy should be undermined, we could consider the enhanced empowerment of ourselves and the recipients of evangelization that would result from a missionary approach employing *both* literacy *and* orality as resources. For there is a real danger in our trying to empower people with the living word of God, while they appropriate simply the power of literacy, and in our neglecting the God present in their own words and on their lips while we offer them an idol.[3]

And now our question becomes simply: How is the word to become flesh and dwell among them? Must it be in an alien tongue and a complex written form? Or can we preach the gospel rather than the Bible, the good news rather than the book, the word rather than the text? Can we be "midwives" to the Spirit rather than calligraphers of the letter, or experts in the law? Can we focus on people's hearts rather than on tablets of stone? Or perhaps, in an inclusive, "both/and" spirit, can we learn to appreciate whatever resources are at our disposal, and value all of the above?

The Gaol and the Goal of Language

"Gaol" is a particularly British form for "jail"; almost all my American students "see" it as a "misprint," because they are unfamiliar with it and because they want "goal" to make sense in the context! But whatever sense they construct for it is different from mine; and if I am the person using my native language, then "my" sense must have some kind of validity!

Can we reasonably consider language to be open-ended and amenable to whatever meanings we impose on it? Is language a tool which we fashion for our own ends? Or need we look further than this view, however appealing it might be? We have two opposing view to consider, as well as the possibility that there might be truth in both.

UNIVERSALISM

The classical Greek philosophy on which much western thinking is based taught that there was a single truth, logic and reason underlying all language; it was universal and universally accessible. The implication here is that no matter what particular language one spoke, full communication was possible since all languages would tap in to the same underlying reality.

Words were the numberless vehicles running on the single universal track of reason, and many of these vehicles were effectively interchangeable. Therefore any sentiment, proposition, or principle, any argument or discussion, could be formulated in any language, translated into any other, and retain its sense in the transition.

This is a comforting and appealing theoretical argument which upholds the unity of truth and logic even in the face of diversity of language. It is an argument that many theologians and missionaries have espoused, at least implicitly. And it is an argument as insidious as it is tempting; for it strips individual languages of their world-creating-and-maintaining functions, it denies to languages their specificity (their unique and culturally determined properties), and it reduces language to its syntactical and grammatical constituents. In other words, such an attractive argument overlooks the semantic component of language: the fact that "she flew off the handle" *cannot* be translated word for word into another language, that it has little to do with unaided—or aided—human flight, and that it remains meaningful whether or not it has a literal equivalent in another language.[4]

PARTICULARISM

Whorf attempted to discredit and disprove the universalistic approach to language by invoking practical examples. He was obviously not going to deny flatly the translatability of ideas, but focusing on language itself he was able to assert that "a change in language can transform our appreciation of the cosmos" and that "each language performs [an] artificial chopping-up of the continuous spread and flow of existence in a different way."

Studies have shown that if people from different cultures and with different languages (as well as all-male or all-female groups) are presented with a chart showing the spectrum from infra-red to ultra-violet, they will "chop up" the spectrum and ascribe names to different colors differently. "Gray" and "brown" are cultural and linguistic constructs: Dutch and French and English see them differently. Similarly, one cannot simply translate "chair" into "chaise" and claim an equivalent notion in French and English; "fauteuil" contains some of the elements associated with the English "chair," just as "chaise" denotes objects not quite the same as a "chair." There is certainly something to be said for Whorf's claim that no two languages describe or itemize the world or relationships in quite the same way.

PRISM OR PRISON?

It is crucial, when translating words or ideas, that the interlocutors share some kind of feedback mechanism by which they can check how their intended communication is actually being received by the other. Without this, major mis-communication may go undetected until too late. I once referred to the third person of the Trinity as "the saving Spirit of God," believing that this offered a more dynamic equivalent than the term "Ghost"—even "Holy" Ghost. But a teacher was interpreting, thought he heard me say "the *seven spirits* of God" (and I had never before used the term "saving Spirit," anyway), and proceeded to translate this theological solecism for the people! I happened to hear him doing this, and since it contributed to the point I was making, I asked him what "the seven spirits of God" meant. He said he had no idea, but I had said it; therefore it must mean something, so he translated it! How many more of our well-intentioned lessons are lost in translation, how often are we completely unaware of what the people think we have said? We have to *learn* to say what we mean, *learn* to pick up what people think we mean, *learn* to hear what people say, and *learn* to check if what we understand is the same as what the speaker meant to say. Language has great potential for the intercommunication of ideas—but it also traps the unwary and causes untold confusion. This being the case, Whorf's observations remain forceful and cautionary.

RULES AND RECIPROCITY

If we are to move beyond a world of subjective meanings, then we must have rules which are known and shared. Each language is a conventional system of shared rules and significations, and if, between two speakers, there is less than a certain minimum number of commonly-held rules or a certain amount of shared meanings, then we have mutual unintelligibility. This is in fact possible between two people who both think they are speaking the same language, even though more noticeable between people who speak quite different languages. At least in the latter case both parties *know* that they do not understand each other; in the former case there may be a shared and dangerous assumption that they do!

Evangelization is communication,[5] and it simply cannot be undertaken at the whim of one party. True communication depends on there being common ground; certainly, one party's "good will," though necessary, is inadequate. Nor can we missionaries naively assume that the gospel can be proclaimed other than in a *specific* language with its own structures, conventions and meanings. It would be literally non-sensical for us to imagine that in order to ensure the adequate transmission of the gospel, all that is required is for other people to be made literate in the language in which we intend to proclaim it! Without some feedback mechanism whereby both parties can check that they are making themselves understood and being understood in turn, language will be no more than babel. Adequate or satisfactory communication between people who do not share a common tongue—a common linguistic system, but also a set of common assumptions about the world, which, as Whorf asserts, differentiates languages—is not possible without concerted hard work on *both* sides of the linguistic divide. Teaching literacy skills in a world-language to people who think and see and judge and pray in a very different language and mentality is *not* going to provide them with automatic facility in the ways of thinking and seeing and judging and praying which characterize the native speakers of the world-language. If the gospel is to be translated—"carried over"—into another culture, then indeed it must be translated—"transformed," "converted," "displaced"—from one linguistic system to another. Without such a fundamental upheaval, of both the messenger and the message, the *meaning* of the gospel in all its richness and depth and subtlety and appropriateness—in a word, its relevance—will remain trapped between the covers of a lifeless text. This is not true evangelization; by itself, without some key and some discussion, without real translation and authentic tradition, bible is no better than babel.

Reciprocity must mean more than turning people into images of ourselves by giving them our language and expecting them to adopt our ways of thinking and acting. Reciprocity must mean that we will receive from others, just as they will receive from us. Reciprocity will result only if we respect the values of others and the presence of God in their lives. So what are we, Christians and missionaries, prepared to receive from others? Do we still in our hearts believe without qualification that we possess the "pearl of great price" and that others are no more than impoverished beggars? In the next chapter we will look at the dynamics of a gift-giving that is reduced to the unilateral patronage of a rich almoner, and when we do we will note the arrogant and supremacist attitudes therein which would put such a patron at odds with the approach of Jesus. Meanwhile perhaps we might note that evangelists—messengers, missionaries, members of the community of believers—who place the brunt of responsibility on the recipients will fail to convince those same recipients that they really value the message they bring. If missionaries are not dedicated to a systematic study of the forms of language of the people they claim to serve, then the word of God, far from being alive and active, far from liberating, far from uplifting and bringing peace, will be dead, or passive, enslaving, depressing and destructive, and will fail to bring joy and hope and heroism because it will simply not be relevant.

Orality and Literacy

THE PEN IS MIGHTIER THAN THE WORD?

A linguistic system, then, must be equipped with the means for assessing and checking the degree of mutual comprehension. Yet it remains possible to use language, deliberately or by default, to conceal or confuse, to evade or prevaricate; and written language is particularly amenable to this linguistic function, since it is fixed, objective, and independent of both speaker/writer and hearer/reader. But because the written form of language does not and cannot engage two interlocutors in reciprocity and the real interchange of information, and relies for its effect on purely linguistic conventions—grammatical, syntactic, and semantic, as well, perhaps, as stylistic—it is inherently less powerful a tool of communication than the spoken word, which, with its redundancy (repetition, interrogation, tone, gesture, emphasis and so on), is extremely efficient for refining and clarifying and affirming what is communicated.

Many people are surprised to hear that the spoken word is in many ways more effective than the written. But that is largely because they are not only well-versed in skills of literacy and thus content to believe that such proficiency is an unmitigated good thing, but are correspondingly undeveloped in skills more appropriate to a non-literate—what we can now call an "oral"—world. And since evangelization very frequently takes place in a context of non-literacy, whether this be illiteracy proper or orality proper, we should surely look at some of the properties of both the "oral mentality" and of orality as it is manifested concretely in cultures.

How often do people refer to the speech of others—especially, as it

happens, where the languages do not have a written form other than perhaps a recent phonetic notation provided by outsiders—as a "dialect"
rather than a "language." I believe this says a great deal about how such
forms of speech are viewed: debased, inferior, non-standard, ephemeral,
insignificant. But of course even if they *were* dialects strictly so-called, they
would not merit such disparaging and inaccurate remarks. Yet the fact that
they are not dialects but languages—unwritten, local, without literate
forms, but systematic, sophisticated and complex—should at least give us
pause to respect their integrity and uniqueness, and to comprehend that
they can *only* be adequately approached on their own terms.

The fact that a language has a written form says nothing about its genius,
except that there must have been an overwhelming need for it to be written
down. Only a few percent of the world's languages have ever had an
indigenous written form, and that is because such a form was simply irrelevant; people, and the society as a whole, could manage quite adequately
with speech and memory! Indeed, a written form of language could be seen
as much as an acknowledgment of the *failure* of a society to marshal and
transmit its knowledge efficiently as it is of its success in coping with such
knowledge. Many of us who have known only a literate culture are dimly
aware, perhaps, of the poverty of our memories; we can always "look it up"
if we need a particular piece of non-experiential knowledge, or we can find
a specialist. Our whole culture is rooted in and quite dependent upon data
banks, reference libraries, experts in information retrieval, and specialists.[6]
And *because* we can use reference books and other literate forms of knowledge, our memories do not need to retain large amounts. Indeed, the mark
of a good academic—an "absent-minded professor"—may be precisely the
ability to tap into a wider range of references than others, and then to assay
the information. Academics may sometimes have very little first-hand experience, and be rather limited in the degree to which they can act directly on
the world, whether in terms of catching trains, hammering nails, fixing
machines, or raising families, telling stories or doing good.

If we persist in thinking of literacy, therefore, as an unequivocal blessing,[7] and of the absence of this particular skill as an unmitigated evil, then
surely we will want to do everything possible to share this essential resource
with others: the illiterate. But note how our very use of language
here—"literacy/illiteracy"—bears out Whorf's observation; we postulate
illiteracy as the opposite of literacy and invest it with pejorative overtones,
since we have already made the assumption that literacy is something good!

We do the same when we speak of "non-believers," "non-Catholics," "non-smokers," "non-combatants," "non-whites," or "non-violent action," thereby making belief, Catholicism, smoking, combat, whites, or violence the "normal," the "standard," the "acceptable," and, implicitly at least, the "good," the "right," and the "true." We need a very careful and radical reppraisal of this sort of attitude, and may begin by taking orality on its own terms, not as the opposite of literacy—the lack of something, the abnormal or the non-standard—but as something positive, powerful, pervasive, popular, and a precious resource which was central to the preaching of Jesus and which we have almost forgotten.

RELIGION AND RELEVANCE

Jesus preached—at times magnetically but always in a memorable, and therefore a relevant way—to people who were largely not "illiterate" but positively "oral." Both the structure of his preaching and the way in which his hearers assimilated knowledge facilitated retention and transmission, as well as interjection and involvement. How often we see Jesus consciously drawing the people into the discourse, and using their replies and observations as the matter for his further teaching! Nowhere do we find—and indeed nowhere does it seem unusual that this is so—that Jesus intends people to take notes, be sure to remember exactly what he says, or to retain his "ipsissima verba" to be used as a precedent or an unequivocal record of his words when arguments arise. Yet clearly Jesus says some enormously important things which are not to be taken lightly or misconstrued. And, equally clearly, there were occasions when the words credited to him by evangelists seem to us ambiguous, or caused disagreement among his hearers. How shall we understand this apparently cavalier attitude?

If we perceive Jesus as a master of an oral style of discourse, and his hearers as proficient interlocutors, versed in the same style and its interpretation, then we can reread the gospels with much profit. But how can we characterize the "oral" style?[8] It is one that appeals directly to the imagination and the memory, to the capacity of the audience for storage and retrieval of information, to certain conventions and rules. It is not dependent, of course, on scribes or secretaries, tape recorders or books; and the skills appropriate to these are not relevant. Rather it both assumes the capacity of the human memory to be quite surprisingly huge (by the current standards of literate, computer-and-book-using, men and women), and it serves to enlarge the memory by testing and feeding it. Orality—or an oral style of learning and communicating—employs many forms of language, some of which are used by literate people, and some of which are either preserved by them in only a rudimentary form, or seem to have been lost forever.

To say that we literates have lost the powers of memory enjoyed by other people—whether Greeks, Romans or those who also employed literacy, or the members of a thousand cultures without it—is to make a virtually meaningless assertion. We may perhaps acknowledge that our memory is not what it was; we may protest that we have a prodigious memory; or we may remain unmoved. But the fact that we are so deeply touched by literacy, both individually and as members of a world which cannot manage without it, is itself explanatory of the fact that we cannot understand what a really powerful memory might mean. And because we are literate, we tend to want to claim that however powerful other people's memories might be or have been, we ourselves can match them by other compensatory skills. It is this idea that I would dearly love to eradicate from the minds and attitudes of missionaries. If I were able to persuade more fellow-missionaries of the riches of orality and memory that have largely remained untapped by us in our efforts to find appropriate and relevant ways of evangelization, and if I could encourage missionaries to approach evangelization—as Jesus did—from an oral rather than a literate starting point, then I would feel exceedingly encouraged about the powers of literacy to look beyond itself, to free itself from some of its more obvious shortcomings, and to become, paradoxically, the supporter of orality!

Jesus used parables, stories, proverbs, and other literary forms. We are aware of this as a fact, but perhaps not of its implications. But when we look at the capacity of the human memory,[9] and when we put this alongside our knowledge of how the people among whom we work as bringers-of-the-good-news pass their time and teach their children and instill principles and broadcast sanctions, then we produce almost a "eureka!-moment"; we are on the threshold of a genuinely new and helpful insight. If we could, as Jesus did, approach the people more explicitly through their oral forms, then evangelization might, at a stroke, become more relevant. If we could see Caribbean "rap" poetry, African "praise-songs," medieval "mystery plays," Indonesian proverbs, rural town criers, Appalachian story-tellers, Eskimo flyting (exchange of insults), black American "just-so" stories, as well as, universally, gossip, as sources and resources for the transmission of the good news, then we would have taken an enormous leap into the heart of other cultures! Let me explain this rather sensational and perhaps reckless claim.

GOSSIP, GOSPEL, AND OTHER GODLY GIFTS

People-in-groups, wherever they are and whatever the era, must succeed in certain tasks or perish. These will include—beyond the obvious provision of nourishment and shelter and the reproduction of the group—both the inculcation of a sense of group-identity and the maintenance of certain standards without which the group will break up or fail to survive. We could look at these two undertakings in concert.

A sense of group-identity can be transmitted in any number of ways, but the one to underline here concerns the sharing of a common past and a common effort. And when people gather to share their commonness and to pass it on to the newer members of the group, then they are about a very serious business. In terms that we have been using already, they are not simply passing the time or indulging in irrelevant and tedious duties. They are manifestly undertaking something extremely important, and are doing so within a relevant group; anyone who is there is there because he or she "belongs," and those who do not "belong" are not there in any significant or systematic way. Now what the people are doing is essentially—given a wonderful variety of forms—telling stories. Story-telling is as old as it is important; those who share stories share history and relevance and aspirations. So where is the preacher-and-teller-of-the-story-of-the-risen-one when these stories are being told?

"Stories" may include great heroic epics,[10] as well as "just-so" stories, reminiscences, proverbs, folk-tales and many other forms. They may be "performed" formally by famous people on special occasions, or shared informally by the whole group at almost any time. Such stories and narratives may be already be known intimately to almost all the assembled group, or surprise by their novelty.[11] They may meet with quiet acceptance or raucous comment, and they may frighten or shame as often as they please and entertain. But all the time, cumulatively, and with great repetition and redundancy, by means of participation and pedagogy, they serve to bind the group together, and to educate the members to the point where they simply cannot forget who they are and the values that they uphold and respect. So where is the missionary, creative sharer, builder-of-the-community-of-faith-in-the-Lord, when these values are exposed and shared?

"Stories" are to oral cultures what laws and injunctions are to literate ones. But the term "story" needs to be expanded if we are to see both the breadth of diversity and the degree of functional similarity between many oral forms. We might not instinctively group together those characters of the middle ages, the troubadours, jongleurs and goliards (itinerant purveyors of news, scandal, and popular songs, all of whom, incidentally, employed music and its rhythms to enhance and recall and transmit what was stored in their memory), with tellers of tales and retailers of proverbs, purveyors of gossip and performers of dumb-shows. But they have a common property in that they highlight the social group by limning its boundaries, by mocking the "deviant" as they underscore the "normal," by appealing to the lubricious and salacious as they subtly point to the righteous, by sanctioning the errant as they reward the loyal, and by informing the community as they form the communal memory. If we could see gossip[12] (referring to the wholesome conversation relevant to the extended family and shared at christenings and weddings and funerals; containing, certainly, elements of prejudice and slander and innuendo, but equally certainly pointing out what the group *disapproves of*), or pop music (recording as well as changing the most characteristic values of the group), or folk tales (showing how virtue is ultimately justified and vice to be resisted), and all the rest, as—implicitly and in rudimentary form perhaps, but not to be neglected for all that—soil in which the gospel might grow, or seeds which might bear good fruit at harvest time, then I think we could converge on what people see as relevant rather than carp and criticize and threaten their world of meaning. If we really looked for "gospel-values"—implicit, subtle or informally presented attitudes containing elements which echo the more explicit values declaimed by Jesus—under the rubric of "storytelling" in oral societies, we could discover such a diversity, across both time and culture, as would not only surprise us but occupy us in adapting the lessons and psychology of Jesus. So where is the missionary, the proclaimer-of-the-good-news-of-Jesus, when people gossip, when jokes evoke wry and ribald laughter, or when communities foregather to hear the comedians and the jesters, the tellers of tales and the singers of songs?[13]

To recapitulate: the multifarious kinds of orality to be found in cultures which use no literate forms help to maintain the identity of the group and serve to teach certain social and moral standards, directly and indirectly, positively and negatively. We literacy-dependent Christians may be blind and deaf to the richness of language which is not tied to literacy. Jesus was extremely sensitive to the oral uses of language, and his whole psychology and pedagogy took advantage of them. Since a majority of the world's people[14] are not literate or minimally so, we missionaries might be gainfully employed in learning more about orality, and about the place and varieties of language in the lives of the people we serve.

I knew some proverbs and tales in my time in West Africa, but I never understood just how much they touched the people's hearts and minds. And yet I know now—by accident or providence—that my words reached out in a special way when clothed in familiar terms and evoking their own wisdom and memories. But how much more there was to be learned, and how poorly I brought the oral gospel to an oral people, or the community of storytellers to the riches of the stories of Jesus.[15]

The activity of evangelization must converge with people's lives as they are being lived, not be a voice crying petulantly in the wilderness. And unless we who bring good news really strive to come closer to the experience of the people, then we will be pathetically crying in a wilderness of our own making. Jesus constantly met people on their own ground and spoke to them in familiar idioms and with memorable figures of speech (and in our final chapter we will look more closely at his approach), allowing himself to be impressed, encouraged, touched and comforted by their integrity and their gestures of hospitality or repentance. In the spirit of Jesus we can discover many, many ways in which the people of oral cultures embody and manifest attitudes or virtues already highly compatible with his preaching. If we neglect to emphasize such attitudes and virtues, we will have nothing on which to build; the degree to which we respect such attitudes and virtues is the degree to which we respect the people. And if we are seen both to respect the people and to be excited at the prospect of sharing the good news we bring, then we might well continue to be relevant, and therefore interesting and worthy of attention.

This is not the place to elaborate on the characteristics of the oral style, but we may recall a few here.[16] I have in fact tried to employ some of them, especially in this chapter; perhaps they will assist in the assimilation of the material in the present section. They include alliteration, repetition, triads (groups of three: phrases, questions, nouns, and so on), and rounding (finishing successive sections with the same words); and there are many others. More important perhaps, in concluding, are some remarks about the effect of an oral perspective on the subject-matter of evangelization.

With an oral mentality and an oral approach, we might be more able to project a living word than a dead letter. There is an ever-present danger of literal-mindedness or formalism when we adopt a literate approach, if it leads us to concentrate on the *text* rather than the *word*. But these are very different indeed; Jesus *spoke,* and his words brought life.[17] He had power over words and spoke "performatively": "you are healed," "your sins are forgiven," "this is my body," and so on. There is a whole theology about the word and the law, the spirit and the letter; but Jesus' magnetism was in his living words. If we reduce this vibrant, direct message to a recitation or a reading, we demean and destroy its efficacy. If people ask for bread, would we give them a stone? If people hunger for a word of life, will we read them a book? And if people need a word that heals, do we thrust a text at them? Bible and text are artifacts that make some sense to a literate person, and none to an oral person; but gospel (good news), word (*logos*), and words (utterances, communication) can speak directly to persons and to hearts. Unless we speak to persons, and listen to hearts that speak, there will be precious little communication, virtually nothing of relevance, and a travesty of evangelization.

Language, Thought, and Reality

ORALITY REVISITED

Now that at least a corner of the vast and largely buried edifice of orality has been uncovered, the issues raised by Sapir and Whorf can be read-dressed. If each literate language be considered as handling reality in a slightly different way, then how should oral languages be considered? Perhaps we have not thought of languages as distinguishable in terms of literate or oral forms, but this is actually a very significant distinction indeed. Scholars are beginning to understand that the shift from orality to literacy represents a profound and fundamental shift in thought, in thinking, and in world-construction.[18] Missionaries born and raised in a literate climate have never experienced such a transition or shift; we took literacy absolutely for granted, as synonymous with education. Consequently, most of us cannot know experientially what the shift might entail. And then there are the millions of people who were born and raised in an oral world, and who have never had reason to make the shift in the other direction, from orality to literacy. So for these too, there is no way of understanding what a literate mentality might entail. But in our day—and increasingly so—hundreds of thousands of people, born in strongly oral environments, are experiencing the trauma of becoming literate; and many others, partially literate through a modicum of schooling, are finding themselves in an environment which has changed in a generation from oral to semi-literate, and which now reflects neither an oral nor a literate world at all adequately. Not surprisingly then, they are confused and disoriented by the change.

If we consider the contemporary "western" world and the short shrift most people give to "illiteracy" (self-righteously imagining it to represent only a deficiency, and with no understanding of the intrinsic power of "orality") we can understand something of the pain of oral peoples. And if we acknowledge that little, very little, is being done to reap the fruits of orality and to fill our cultural barns with them,[19] then we might, appropriately, be a little shamefaced.

Can a person socialized in a highly literate culture ever understand someone with no experience of literacy and with skills rooted in orality? The answer has to be a both/and answer. A person who speaks only English *can*—but only proleptically—understand a person whose language is Cantonese. That is, not today, and not without enormous toil and commitment; not without systematic study, which implies motivation, which leads back to . . . relevance. In the short term, English-speaker and Cantonese-speaker may each imagine he or she can understand the other; but much apparent understanding proves to be incomplete or quite misconceived. Similarly, "literate" and "oral" persons might imagine that they understand each other, but with the same consequences as for the English and Cantonese speakers. Where evangelization is involved, "hit-and-miss" understanding is of course quite inadequate.

When considering the assertions of Sapir and Whorf, we must apply them not only to different (literate) languages, but to languages distinguished by other properties, including, especially important for our consideration here, those of orality. According to Whorf, speakers of different languages are prejudiced—by virtue of their language itself—in relation to each other:

Every language and every well-knit technical sub-language incorporates certain points of view and certain *patterned resistance* to widely divergent points of view.

And, more radically, Sapir:

> It is almost as though at some period in the past, the unconscious mind of the race had made a hasty inventory of experience, committed itself to a premature *classification that allowed of no revision,* and saddled the inheritors of its language with a science that they no longer believed in nor had the strength to overthrow. [Therefore] the worlds in which different societies live are distinct worlds, not the same world with different labels attached. (My italics throughout)

Evangelization must come to terms with such insistent argument. If we adopt a simple dichotomy, we could say that either we can "translate" the gospel into any and all cultures, or we cannot. But the reality is far more complex. In the first place it would always be a temptation for us to *think* we were "translating" when in fact we were simply dictating and failing to check on the message as received. But, secondly, I think we must adopt the both/and approach, acknowledging that with great effort translation *can* happen, but that there will always be elements that are not quite translatable yet might perhaps pass from one culture to another. We tend not to translate "nuance," "naive," or "finesse," for example; yet they have passed into our language. But because they are now part of "our" language, they no longer mean precisely what they mean in French or to a French speaker; the *nuances* are slightly different. So we will not be *naive,* and can use our language with both *finesse* and meaning, if we remember the differences!

It is always possible to set out to cross linguistic divides. We may never succeed completely in understanding a speaker of another language, but, realistically, we know that we never succeed in understanding *anyone* completely: such is the inscrutability and uniqueness of the individual. But the lesson for us missionaries to learn is that when the divide is the oral/literate divide, it is we who must make the move; we literates need to equip ourselves with oral skills, or at least a working knowledge of orality. The oral person who becomes literate does not immediately forget an impressive range of oral skills which are also carriers of meaning and points of reference; that person's world continues to rely for its permanence on the oral underpinnings. On the principle that whoever wills the end wills the means, the literate Christian who wishes to appeal to others in terms of their life experience simply must undertake to be schooled in oral skills; otherwise there is no solid common ground on which to build new communities of belief, united in the living word of Jesus.

CONCLUSIONS: THEORETICAL, PRACTICAL, PASTORAL

There remains only a little space in which to make some observations and urge personal thought and study.

Parables, especially the parables of the kingdom, not only provide access to what should become a Christian mentality, but are wonderfully appropriate to an oral culture. They embody, as it were, the good news. They provide a practical and relevant approach to other cultures and to people without deep awareness of who Jesus was, because those were indeed among the original functions of the parables. To teach, not through catechism nor law nor principle, but through story and from life, is Jesus' own way. It is surely not chance that brings missionaries into contact with people so similar in oral mentality to the crowds in Jesus' day. How profligate we would be, to neglect his pedagogy in favor of texts and rules that bind and kill. The beauty of parables is that they can be understood—in many ways, and at many levels, but understood nevertheless—by those who have ears. And the good news must pass through the ears of people and be heard by them according to their own genius and capacity.[20] Every missionary can tell the stories of Jesus and listen to the stories of the people. And every missionary can introduce Jesus and cultures to each other, simply and unpompously, before stepping back in wonder, at the outcome.

In our day there are numerous difficulties, discussions and disagreements, between and among missionaries and theologians, about how best to undertake evangelization. We cannot solve or even address all the problems, but we can tell the story of Jesus, and we can tell the stories that Jesus told. Such an apparently simple approach may have been overlaid by dogmatic and catechetical considerations, to the point where we are in grave danger of announcing something other than the good news of Jesus. The doctrine and the catechesis is ready to be found in the oral gospel and in its written form, and to be applied to oral peoples.

Continuing study of some of the other issues raised so far would convince us of the special relationship which exists within the triad formed by language, thought, and reality. In drawing our attention to the fact that any given language is not totally free—granted its potential for absorption and expansion—to express all theoretically possible ideas and relationships, Sapir and Whorf were reminding us that we are all rooted in our culture, with its patterns of thinking, of doing, and indeed of seeing the world. Such is the interconnectedness of language and thought that we hardly think about the problem of the limits of language; we commonly assume that we can say anything and reach out and indeed grasp the real world through our language. There is nothing wrong with this; we rarely *need* to formulate questions, unless we are philosophers, or linguists, or indeed bearers of the word—a word that is not only living and challenging, but "realized," "incarnated" we might almost say, in a particular language. But once we do begin to ask questions about the worlds created and maintained by language, the diverse viewpoints embodied in different languages, and the power of language to shape our thinking, then we find that evangelization is indeed a marvelous and specifically human challenge, as daunting as it is exciting.

"Language determines perception" is about as strong a form of the unformulated "Whorfian hypothesis" as it is possible to construct. It is most unlikely that Whorf himself would have subscribed to it *in that form.* But what about a both/and approach? And what if we stand it on its head? Is there any light shed, either by the proposition as it stands, or by the inverted proposition: "perception determines language"? From what we have seen, it is clear both that there is a special interrelatedness between language and perception, and that whatever this is in specific terms, it carries considerable implications for those proclaiming a word and attempting to modify and broaden the perceptions of others. Certainly the processes of evangelization must succeed in reaching other people's worlds —their language, their thought, and their reality—or there will have been no communication, and therefore no good news.

Evangelization is an activity not for a vacuum nor for a laboratory, but for a specific society. Once we concentrate on a context we may learn to see both how the speakers within that context chop up experience differently from ourselves, and how similar are our respective ways, at times. We can learn from the differences just as from the similarities in our thinking. We can come to acknowledge that other people's worlds are as real as our own, and that they will often find us no less odd than we are tempted to think of them.

The fact that the Sapir/Whorf hypothesis is untestable does not invalidate it. And if we really follow up some of its implications, then those of us who have spent some time in other cultures will probably experience another of those "eureka!-moments" that give us encouragement to continue.

No language has ever proved incapable of adapting to demands made on it. Sometimes these may be great, and sometimes languages may undergo damaging change. But languages are living, and therefore they are changing, since to live is to change. The good news of Jesus *can* find a setting in which it makes sense, or it can be declaimed prematurely in a community that simply cannot understand it. To be a good missionary is to be sensitive to—among other things—the functions and constraints of language-in-society in order to gauge when and how the word of God can best be transmitted. The task can be done; but it can be done badly and produce confusion, rather more easily than well and with enlightenment. Missionaries should know the difference.

Language need not imprison thinking and obfuscate reality. But such is its power, it will do these things if we make it, or allow it to. And such is its power, it can be used both to give and to take, to liberate and to enslave, to teach and to indoctrinate. Language has enormous potential for stimulating and freeing thought, for illuminating reality, for transmitting deep insights and evoking profound emotions. Language gives wings to thought and challenges us to change and to action. How wonderful that we speak so explicitly of the *word*—the communication within the Godhead, the utterance of the Creator who "said . . . and so it was," the message of God, spoken for all people and all times—*who was made flesh and dwelt among us.* We were not given tablets of stone, formalized and immutable texts, or meaningless laws, ridden with legalese, but a living, warm, active word, conceived of God and born uniquely in the hearts of all who can hear.

So are there any convincing arguments for our not learning local languages yet continuing to claim that we bring good news? Is it defensible for us to walk into other cultures without being deeply committed to learning how the people make sense of the world? Can we rest without questioning our own assumptions and categories? And are we ready for the long haul, once we realize that people do not only live in other places, far away or relatively near, but other worlds-of-meaning which only impinge on ours to the degree to which we embrace them?

Notes and Bibliography

1. The most easily available book of Whorf's essays is *Language, Thought and Reality,* Cambridge, Mass., M.I.T. Press, 1966. His ideas are discussed in virtually all introductions to general linguistics.

2. J.L. Austin talks about the "performative" aspect of language in *How To Do Things With Words,* Harvard, Mass., Harvard University Press, 1962.

3. In the book *The Myth of Christian Uniqueness,* New York, Orbis Press, 1988, there is an essay by Wilfred Cantwell Smith, "Idolatry in Comparative Perspective," pp. 53–68. I found this stimulating, challenging, and very relevant to our purpose here.

4. The notion of "dynamic equivalence," whereby terms or phrases are translated with an eye to total context, is probably familiar. We have to find *meaningful* translations as we take the Bible from one culture to another. How might we translate "lamb of God" to people who live in Arctic wastes? Could we ever think of something like "pig of God" for people who live in Pacific pig-cultures, or does this offend our own sensibilities to the point where we protest? Again, some languages may not start a sentence with a demonstrative ("this"), but state the substantive first ("bottle"); thus the English "this is a bottle" is rendered "the bottle it is this one." Now for those who accept the real presence of Jesus in the eucharist, there is a theological problem if we raise *bread* ("this") but identify it *first* as "*body*"; we think of the power of conse-cration as effecting the change *from* "this (bread)" *to* "my body." Languages that say "my body it is this one" leave us with a problem of identification (is "this" actually *bread,* or *body?*). There are very many other examples which make translation a theological and semantic minefield. But that is not the last word; minefields can be negotiated in various ways.

5. Elizabeth Brewster and her (now deceased) husband wrote a splendid article on this topic for the *International Bulletin of Missionary Research.* It is "Language Learning Is Communication, Is Ministry," 1982:160ff.

6. Marshall McLuhan was the guru of media studies, and has produced some highly informative material. Particularly helpful, if sometimes dense, is *The Gutenberg Galaxy,* New York, Signet Books, 1962; and more accessible is *Understanding Media,* New York, Signet Books, 1964.

7. Ivan Illich will surely shake us out of any complacency we may have about the unmitigated blessings of literacy. We have already referred to his work, worth reading for ideas, passion, and sometimes excellence.

8. A modest but most helpful book is Walter Ong's *Orality and Literacy,* New York, Methuen, 1981. This is a fine survey of the area I tread on here.

9. The first and thus the best history of the art of memory in English is by Frances A. Yates, published in 1966. It is available now, *The Art of Memory,* in

an ARK Edition, London, Routledge and Kegan Paul, 1984; and it is eye-openingly amazing!

10. Three references here to the "greats." Albert Lord's *The Singer of Tales* shows how Balkan epic-singers learned their prodigious feats of memory, and how they produced "creative-memory" renditions for hours on end. His work was inspired by the classicist Milman Parry who worked on the Homeric epics and their transmission. That work is available as *The Making of Homeric Verse: The Collected Papers of Milman Parry,* edited by Adam Parry, published at Oxford by Clarendon Press, 1971. The third reference is to the work of Vladimir Propp, particularly his *Morphology of the Folktale,* Texas, University of Texas Press, 1968. Here Propp argues that all folk-tales of a certain type share a common structure which can be discovered beneath the variations. This insight is used too by Kelber (see n. 17) when discussing the parables in Mark and helps explain how they might be memorized and retold in their integrity.

Helen Waddell's book, *The Wandering Scholars,* London, Constable Co., 1927/1987, is a study of the "Vagantes" whose repertoire of songs and poetry was prodigious: another indication of how much a memory trained to deal with oral rather than written information can retain and transmit.

Isidore Okpewho has been studying the epic (and myth, too) in Africa. His book is *The Epic in Africa,* New York, Columbia University Press, 1979.

11. A good story-teller, especially of "creative" stories, will presumably refine the stories and then tell them in several locations; it would be less than sensible to give one's best stories only a single telling! Similarly, I imagine that Jesus would have told the same parable on several occasions. Each telling is special; there is no such thing as "the original" for a story-teller, since each rendition is original, though slightly different. Perhaps our search for the "original" occasion of Jesus' stories or parables is misdirected; for if each has something special to tell, and none need have absolute priority, we can approach them with a certain freshness.

12. "Gossip" derives from "God" + "sip/sib[ling]"; thus it refers both to "God-talk" and to "family/familiar-talk." A recent book deals with it, though largely from a literary perspective. Still, there are some useful observations for the present context too. See Patricia Spacks, *Gossip,* Chicago, University of Chicago Press, 1985.

13. Apart from the references already given, there is a stimulating recent work by a missionary, Kevin B. Maxwell. It is *Bemba Myth and Ritual: The Impact of Literacy on an Oral Culture,* New York (and Frankfurt and Berne), Peter Lang, 1983. Maxwell shows how literacy brings a new way of thinking (one that leads away from the mentality of Jesus or Paul as much as it leads toward the Bible or the text).

14. See *The World Christian Encyclopedia,* edited by David Barrett, Oxford, Oxford University Press, 1982, Table 22, p. 781, and more recently his "Status of Global Mission, 1987, in Context," in *International Bulletin of Missionary Research,* 11 (1) 1987:25. Barrett gives these figures: 29.8% of Christian adults and 66.7% of all adults in the world are not literate. This indicates that (at most, depending on how "literacy" is understood) seven out of ten Christians and one out of three adults globally do not operate with literacy skills; how *do* they operate, and how well acquainted are we, with their skills?

15. A simple example: a Mende proverb (Sierra Leone) says "An empty sack cannot stand" (beki wopu ee gu a lola). This may "mean" something very simple when translated literally; but what it "really" means is demonstrated by the context. It is said when a person is asked to work harder, or is justifying his or her exhaustion; if there is no *food* inside a person, then that person cannot function. It really has nothing at all to do with bags; it is about bodies.

16. A competent roundup of the characteristic of the oral style, in respect of the written gospel, is D. Rhoads and D. Michie, *Mark as Story,* Philadelphia, Fortress Press, 1982.

17. I think one of the most creative books of recent years, dealing with the spoken word of Jesus and of Paul, and the transition from their speech to the written gospels and epistles, is Werner Kelber's *The Oral and the Written Gospel,* Philadelphia, Fortress Press, 1983. This had a profound effect on my thinking.

18. Anthropologist Jack Goody has pursued—not unchallenged—some of the most ambitious and rewarding work in the field of orality and literacy. He has much to teach us missionaries. Try *Literacy in Traditional Societies,* Cambridge, Cambridge University Press, 1968, and *The Logic of Writing and the Organization of Society,* Cambridge, Cambridge University Press, 1986.

19. *The Gospel of Solentiname,* in four small volumes, by Ernesto Cardenale, New York, Orbis Press, 1982, shows how a small Christian community shared the word of God and discovered the riches and applications therein. It is truly amazing how the good news comes alive among the people as they reflect and pray together. What can happen in Nicaragua can and should happen in Christian communities elsewhere.

20. William J. Bausch has written on the theme of storytelling and provides examples and practical advice for those who would like to exploit this potential of the minister's trade. See *Storytelling: Imagination and Faith,* Connecticut, Twenty-Third Publications, 1984. Also on stories as containing "gospel values," see Rosemary Haughton's *Tales from Eternity: The World of Fairy Tales and the Spiritual Search,* New York, Seabury Press, 1973.

Four

Gifts, Guile, and the Gospel

It has been claimed that "the gift is never free." If so, then how can the missionary prevent evangelization becoming moral blackmail? Is it possible to present salvation as a unmerited free gift of God? Can we accept in principle that people may decline the "gift" of the gospel?

"Unpacking" the Gift

A CAUTIONARY TALE

It's easy enough to imagine the scene, a scene that has been played on millions of television sets in recent years . . . : The explorers are hanging little mirrors and plastic combs, lengths of cloth and strings of beads, a knife and a hardened steel axe, on the branches of trees in the Brazilian forest. They know that there are people around, but they cannot see them, for the people are afraid and unaccustomed to contact. The explorers are trying to entice the hidden men and women with the gifts they bring, and to establish contact . . . The next morning, having withdrawn overnight, the explorers return, creeping through the undergrowth, to the previous day's scene. Have the gifts been accepted? Will there be any contact, the beginnings of communication, today . . . ?

The Kreen Akrore are a Brazilian jungle people whose name translates clumsily as "The Tribe that Hides From Man" (the title of a television documentary), and the explorers in this particular case never did gain more than a tantalizing glimpse of buttocks disappearing in the trees. Some of the gifts were touched, examined. But almost without exception, they were not "accepted"; and the explorer and his camera crew never did embark upon a relationship with these silent people . . .

We missionaries do not perhaps creep silently into other people's worlds; but we venture, and we bring gifts. We hope they will be accepted —whatever they may be—and we feel that they are worthy and useful gifts.

Sometimes they are touched, examined. But how often are they *not* really "accepted," assimilated into the lives of their intended recipients? How often would people *like* to decline, but struggle for an appropriate way? How often do we fail to notice their discomfort, or dismiss it through our rationalizations? How aware are we of the "grammar" of gift-giving and gift exchange? And what does all this indicate of the nature of mission, the agenda of the missionary, the freedom of the potential recipients, and the meaning of the messages transmitted between the well-intentioned giver and the potential receiver?

ORIGINS, ETYMOLOGY, IMPLICATIONS

"Gift-exchange" can be seen as a sociological category, but it is also rather like a lens through which we may look at relationships between missionaries and local people. In fact I find it so illuminating and helpful that I believe it worth examining in some detail. But lest we too quickly assume that we know pretty well what the issues are, perhaps we should start at the very beginning and check the dictionary and the anthropological record for information and examples.

The English word "gift" derives from Old Norse, through Old English and Middle English, and has common derivatives in Dutch and German. Originally it meant "payment for a wife," and, in the plural, "wedding." But one of its cognates in Middle Dutch (*gift*) and in Old High German meant, in the feminine form, "gift," and in the neuter, "poison"; and in Middle English one of the meanings of "gift" was "something given to corrupt, a bribe." Bribes make me think of blackmail, and looking up that word I find that "mail" refers to "speech" or "agreement," and also to "payment, tax, rent, tribute"; and "black" is not "evil" or "wicked," but derives from Gaelic and means "protect" or "cherish." And blackmail is: "[Historically], a tribute formerly exacted from small owners in the border districts of England and Scotland, by freebooting chiefs, in return for immunity from plunder"; so here we have a "forced gift," given, or more properly forcibly exacted, for the privilege of freedom, peace, or being left alone. Our brief excursus into the Shorter Oxford Dictionary thus rewards us with notions of "price," "marriage payment," "poison," "blackmail" and "agreement." It may well be true that not all of these senses are current in English today (though actually I will at least refer to them again); but that simply illustrates my point, that it takes two (or more) to make a gift, and that what is understood by one party may not be what is understood by the other. Furthermore, if gift exchange is open to misunderstandings within one culture, then *across cultures* it could easily lead to major misapprehensions and incorrect assumptions.[1]

SOCIAL ASPECTS OF GIFT EXCHANGE

One striking characteristic of human beings everywhere—and one which an imaginary extraterrestrial being could not fail to notice—is that they exchange gifts. Such apparently spontaneous interaction occurs in all but the most abject poor. And even then, the *desire* to exchange, to offer, to be accepted, is not eradicated.

It may be thought that animals too exchange gifts; and we might follow this up by examining which animals are involved, and under what circumstances the gift exchange seems to operate. But one thing is sure; in spite of the apparent spontaneity, gift-giving and gift-receiving are as "rule-governed" as are our old friends chess and football. It was when he perceived the strength of the "rules" that Marcel Mauss was able to observe that "the gift is never free"—something we may consider as we pursue this subject.[2]

In order to understand—and that includes being able to account for and explain occurrences, as well as knowing what is appropriate or expected in given circumstances—we would have to ask questions such as: Who gives gifts (in a particular society)? When are they given? Why? And then: Who does not give gifts? What kind of gifts are unacceptable or refused or not given? And perhaps most important: Where is "power," in specific situations of gift-giving and gift-receiving?

If behavior is a manifestation of underlying belief, just as spoken language is a manifestation of an underlying set of grammatical rules, then what might an external act of gift-giving reveal about underlying expectations and constraints? And if we begin to formulate some answers to questions such as these, are we not close to accepting Mauss' dictum that "the gift is never free"?

Before we advance further, just one note of warning: if gift exchange does turn out to be "rule-governed," then it is open to interpretation, just as is any other rule-governed behavior. And if we can misinterpret what someone says, or what a chess player or a football player intends, then all the more should we acknowledge how very easy it is to interpret another's gift giving with the wrong set of rules, and to produce situations of severe mis-communication. What is the *meaning* of the bunch of red roses that a man brings a woman? How can we understand the *indebtedness* that results from a gift received? What, for instance, may be the nature of marriage payments made in other cultures than our own, by the bridegroom's family and accepted by the bride's? What might be the significance of the part played by families as moral units, buttressing the fragile marriage between two young people? Clearly there are many conceivable answers, many possibilities to be considered, and much room for (deliberate or unintended) misunderstandings.

Toward a Theory of Gift Exchange

SYSTEMATIZATION

Marcel Mauss (1872–1950) was a person of great learning, and from his enormous reading he assembled a huge dossier of case-histories on behavior from many cultures. He set out to contextualize and compare the characteristic patterns, slowly making some sense of hitherto meaningless or bizarre behavior; and the result was published in *The Gift*. Noticing that *obligation* appeared as a constant in gift-giving behavior, he asked: "What is the principle whereby the gift received has to be repaid?" and "What 'force' or 'power' is there in the thing given which compels the recipient to make a return?" And Mauss was able to tease out a general pattern which disclosed a surprisingly widespread *system* of behavior and values (or "belief in action"). Far from a spontaneous or *ad hoc* mechanical transfer of goods and services, gift exchange is seen to be *patterned behavior embodying clear moral values;* it creates and maintains personal relationships, not simply between private individuals, but between groups and between 'moral persons' or statuses, as we shall explain.

GIFTS AND ECONOMIC EXCHANGE

We probably think we know perfectly well the difference between gift exchange and economic behavior, and we are quite sure that there is a difference. But western capitalism and *laissez-faire* individualism are part of a system into which many of us were born—and there *was* life, gift exchange and economic behavior long before the eighteenth century and quite independent of the west. So, before we look too closely at the logic and morality of gift-giving in many cultures, we would do well to examine the various notions associated with it.[3]

In the west we are used to the glorification of individualism, "private enterprise," and impersonal transactional systems. *Laissez-faire*—the doctrine of unrestricted freedom in commerce, especially for private interests —tends to give little or no consideration to persons or relationships, but only to commerce. Prices are fixed, and the goal of "business" is "sale" or "purchase." Everything has its "price," and "money talks." But though the wheels of industry may run smoothly, human relationships tend to suffer. We live in a culture where, in order to transact "business," we need not one but two or more "major credit cards" or other multiple forms of identification—and mere "identification" cards are of themselves insufficient! Our transactions are computerized and facilitated by plastic rectangles, not personalized and facilitated by human interaction. "Commerce" is a hungry deity that devours persons and grows fat on "transactions." The world of western commerce is a world of anonymity and isolation, individualism and technology. Telephones and Telex machines, speculation and "futures," interest rates and Dow Jones, characterize our economic sphere of action.

And then there are gifts. Gifts tend to be notionally and emotionally segregated from our "economic behavior" and to occupy an area of life marked by freedom and intimacy, human relationships and non-competitiveness. We like to think of being surprised by gifts and surprising others, or of allowing gifts to "speak a thousand words." Gifts, we think, should be spontaneous. We say of one who offers an unimpressive gift that it's not so much the gift as the thought behind the gift . . . and so on. But is our gift-giving so pure and "non-economic" when we have grown to expect gifts for birthdays or other specific occasions, when we feel cheated or insulted when our gift is not reciprocated, when the gift we do receive seems insignificant or insulting, or when we feel obligated to give gifts in order to keep up appearances or "because it is expected" or "because it's good for business"? What kind of spontaneity is there in the gift of roses made by a contrite spouse, or the gift that cannot be refused or repaid and binds the recipient to the donor as a debtor? How easily and subtly can a "gift" become "blackmail" or "hush money," payoff or payola? What kind of language do we speak with our gifts, offered against the backdrop of a western capitalist ethos? What is the *moral* value of a "gift-certificate" that can be exchanged at the whim of the recipient for something the donor never thought of; or even of cash, that "all purpose" commodity, which may so easily contain nothing of the giver? And is the language of our own gift exchange the same language as others use? Do our gifts speak unequivocally what we want them to say, and do we receive the donor's message as unambiguously as we receive the donor's gifts? With the suspicion that there may be some discrepancies here, and that therefore our interpretations of others' behavior may be wide of the mark, we move on.

The Logic of Gift Exchange

In his *Argonauts of the Western Pacific* (1922), Bronislaw Malinowski, the "father" of modern participant observation and ethnography, identified a scale of gift exchange among the Trobriand Islanders, ranging from "real barter" to "pure gift."[4] The first was understood to epitomize "commerce" and self-interest, while "pure gift" was held to manifest disinterestedness and altruism, through spontaneity and simplicity. Other people have imagined that "primitive gift exchange" (being too difficult to interpret otherwise) is an archaic economic system which forces people to circulate necessary goods, so that ultimately everyone gets what is "needed." In such a view, later and more sophisticated peoples would develop organized trading and a "rational" approach to economics.

Mauss accepted neither of these views. He emphasizes repeatedly that gift exchange in "other" cultures is *both* self-interested and disinterested. But gift exchange is also institutionalized—that is, patterned into expected forms of behavior that persist over time and involve people in relationships —and not simply "private," much less totally "spontaneous," and certainly not "simple." There may indeed be exchange between specific individuals, but Mauss is talking primarily about "moral persons" and not so-called "private" individuals. Indeed, our familiar notion of a "private" individual is very different from the notion of the socially responsible person in other societies. For Mauss, a "moral person" is an incumbent of a status position—a "father," "mother," "wife," "husband," "chief," "child," "daughter," "blacksmith," "priest," and so on.

All societies, declared Mauss, are able to address and meet their economic needs; they do not need some kind of stereotyped gift exchange as an alternative. There are marketplaces in which goods of equal value or worth are *bartered* and goods of unequal value or worth are *traded*. Thus, it is characteristically economic behavior when one person "gives" another a bunch of bananas and "receives" a couple of fish; this is the essence of economic exchange, and it is not to be confused with gift exchange, properly so-called. And, again, it is economic behavior when one person, after a great deal of interaction with another, hands over several raffia cloths and receives a pig. Bananas for fish constitutes the exchange of items of equal value—they may be classed as "perishables." Raffia cloths and pigs are of unequal value—imperishable and dissimilar. But they are of roughly equal worth inasmuch as a person with pigs may gain prestige just as one with raffia cloths does. And depending upon "market forces"—availability, time spent in labor, ease of replacement—a "price" will be negotiated in an economic fashion (that is, arranging for the allocation and distribution of scarce resources), and unlike the straight barter or direct exchange of perishables.

Whether such negotiations are direct, indirect, or delayed, whether they appear to the outsider—in some of their aspects—to be similar or identical to the outsider's perceptions of gift exchange, they are in fact very different from gift exchange because differently motivated, differently patterned, and differently understood by those involved. In non-western societies economic behavior is still characterized by "human" interaction—as indeed it remains in rural areas in the west. It is not impersonal, and it does contribute to the building up of relationships. But still that does not make it "gift exchange," even though we may think such characteristics mark off gift exchange from other forms of social behavior. But it does make it something other than pure economics, since there is no such thing as pure economics divorced from human interaction.

Rather than seeing relaxed economic exchange in other societies as gift exchange, we might note that in our own western cultures economic transactions have simply become dehumanized. They, too, "should" be marked by cordiality since they seem to be about the interaction of humans. But both the cordiality and the humanness have often been sacrificed on the altar of profit and efficiency, not to mention the more recently erected altar of rationalization. The result of this is that what in other societies coexists in harmony—namely *both* economic exchange *and* gift exchange—has become in the west separated and polarized, with the result that economics tends to pride itself on self-interest, contract, and profit, leaving gift exchange to carry the responsibility for expressing relatedness, spontaneity and altruism.

In the virtual absence of such a dichotomy, "traditional" social systems, says Mauss, exhibit a *continuum* of behavior which *includes and merges* what people in the west try to keep separate: purely economic behavior and institutionalized gift exchange.

THE MORALITY OF GIFT EXCHANGE

If it is wrong for us to judge as "economic" behavior what is infinitely more nuanced and complex, what might be our approach—as missionaries—to some of the behavior we encounter in other cultures? Mauss' insights about the structuring of gift exchange gives us a way of understanding what is "rule-governed" and systematic, provided we address the code itself and try to solve the "puzzle" on its own terms.

First and foremost: people involved in the exchange of gifts are connected in *relationships,* and these may endure throughout the life of the parties. One cannot lightly enter into reciprocal arrangements, nor casually break them; matters of honor, prestige and self-respect are intimately tied up in ongoing gift exchange. One party does not shower repeated and unsolicited gifts on the other, nor does one party relax into a comfortable position as a recipient. The "rules"—unwritten, possibly even unstated, but certainly present and morally binding—indicate approximately when and in what fashion gifts shall be made. Yet Mauss also pointed out incisively how gift-giving could become a manifestation of power and control, if not regulated: "Charity wounds [the one] who receives, and our whole moral effort is directed towards suppressing the unconscious harmful patronage of a rich almoner." Here is an assertion well worth serious thought and discussion by missionaries, used as they are to being "givers," and perhaps too uncritically prepared to accept the adage "neither a borrower nor a lender be," not to mention the out-of-context biblical injunction that it is "better to give than to receive."

Second, then, gift-exchange is *encoded,* and the code can only be cracked by the sensitive and informed investigator. Context and *dramatis personae* are crucial. Not every gift that is offered and accepted is a manifestation of a healthy institutionalization within a given society; there will always be some room for manipulation, exploitation and inequity. But bearing that in mind, we should also be aware of the fact that much gift exchange is as carefully orchestrated as the "Pastoral" Symphony, and as minutely choreographed as any "Swan Lake."

Third, the gift, as Mauss discovered, is in a real sense *an extension of the donor;* it embodies something of the personality or the "spiritual essence" of that person. If one person invests another—by means of a gift—with his or her very essence, then respect for the gift, and then reciprocity, become necessary and understandable. The giver is, almost physically, in the possession of the receiver. Though this may sound somewhat far-fetched, it is comprehensible if we understand that the world is not divided up into "persons" and "things"; such a division may be familiar to us but it is of course a "construct." In many societies, "things" are attached to "persons," and there is no absolute discontinuity between them. Since the person and the object given are already in relationship, it follows that the exchange of gifts creates strong and lasting bonds between persons.

And now perhaps we can see that in our own experience, where the ideas I have been talking of are fractured, we have made an *opposition* between economic or contractual behavior on the one hand, and the gift on the other; and we have created a rift between persons and things. The "gift" as understood in western cultures is our own recent invention; the gift as studied by Mauss—which he called a series of "prestations"—can only be understood as part gift, part loan, part pledge.[5]

THE MECHANICS OF GIFT EXCHANGE

What may appear as a simple, free gift from one person to another may be just that . . . almost. For what we see in the donation and the receipt is only part of a wider scene. And in that wider scene are to be found expectations, obligations, concerns—in short, the stuff of human interaction and possibly relationships.

When we look beyond the individual to that person's *status* as wife, child, father and so on, we often note that the individual is really acting on behalf of a group or in virtue of social constraints which dictate the mode of transaction or relationship. And when we consider the "gift," we have to broaden our categories to include not only material objects but offices, reproductive rights, filiation rights, entertainments and services of various kinds. This is what Mauss found, and which, when referring to lifelong or ongoing reciprocal moral relationships, he called "total prestations."

Social life—from one single perspective—can be seen as a set of obligations and expectations, along with sanctions. Mauss isolated a set or group of three:

—the obligation to GIVE;
—the obligation to RECEIVE;
—the obligation to REPAY.[6]

By looking at these obligations, individually and as a set, we can now make sense of otherwise strange behavior, but perhaps more importantly we can understand the mechanics of our own interactions with people in other cultures, and appreciate *why* they react in certain ways, and how we, often inadvertently, trample on their expectations and their sensibilities.[7]

THE OBLIGATION TO GIVE

This applies not just to one party, the "initiator," the "superior," the one who can "afford" to be "generous"; it applies to *everyone* who wants to be and remain in relationship. Unless we give, we cannot be "received." Unless we give, we remain centered on ourself rather than open to the community, and unless we give, then ultimately we will not receive, and thus remain isolated. People in western societies, with their glorification of individualism, may believe themselves to be independent and in no need of giving or receiving. But people in western societies also have enormous problems of isolation, alienation, loneliness and suicide. No, the obligation to give is binding on all who look beyond individualism to community.

Giving initiates chains of indebtedness and bonds of reciprocity. Gift-giving reinforces self-giving and strengthens relationships. The refusal to give, in tightly-knit societies, may be tantamount to an act of war! Those who have but do not give will not only lose respect but will be aware that witchcraft accusations and blame for unsolved mischief will be laid at their door—effective enough sanctions against overweening individualism!

THE OBLIGATION TO RECEIVE

If giving is an activity intended to open up relationships, then the corollary is that the gift must be accepted. Not to accept may be an act of war! Not to accept may at least be a statement of unwillingness to be in relationship, but the situation is obviously more complicated than that; for the "giver" is initially in a superior position to the intended recipient, first because the giver opens up the situation and initiates the relationship, but also because the receiver becomes thereby indebted to the giver. Here is where "power" can be seen as the underlying language of gift exchange.

Indebtedness is of course no bad thing; it is even the core of the "message" of gift exchange. People *want* to be indebted to others, precisely because this indicates relationship. But no one wants to be indebted to *everyone,* and to have no one in his or her debt. Debt can be as crippling as it is potentially liberating, and if the debtor has no resources with which to repay, then a dilemma is created. Refusal to receive, as we stated, can be interpreted as a very negative act, yet being prevailed upon to accept another's pledge or service or object may be the last straw . . .

THE OBLIGATION TO REPAY

Repayment must be perceived as at least *possible,* even though it may not be expected immediately. Indeed in some cases, to try to reciprocate too quickly is a sure sign that the gift was not valued highly. Sometimes one is required to remain "in debt" for a lengthy period, as an acknowledgment of the particular relationship. But whoever is in long-term debt to one "partner" (I do not want to say "creditor" since it smacks of bailiffs and contracts, and will take us back to western, rational, economic theory) will normally expect to have other partners in situations of indebtedness.

A little reflection will show that, though there is a system, and though it may seem very "neat," nevertheless it is full of potential for manipulation and "rule-breaking." Not everyone is simon-pure, and life would be rather tedious if all the rules were kept all the time! So we can see possible use and abuse of the system. A giver may indeed exploit a recipient's reluctance to refuse, thus instigating an unwanted relationship—characterized as "blackmail," "persuasion," or "seduction." In such cases, gifts are indeed "poison," as our etymological survey revealed.

Gift-giving, ostensibly a sign of self-giving, is now revealed as an effective means of *masking* the very thing it should disclose, or, more subtly, it may be used to provoke shame in the recipient, as the story of Wakasilele illustrates:

Wakasilele's friend from another village presented him with a large pig. Wakasilele is a "big man," a tough, stony-faced leader with a ferocious temper and a haughty pride. His friend was not a "big man," but he left Wakasilele speechless with emotion when he gave him the pig. "Why is he being given the pig?" I asked. "Because his friend is angry with him," I was told. The friend had earlier brought Wakasilele some shell-fish from the coast, but the latter had churlishly spurned the gift. The giver was ashamed, insulted and indignant. To point out to Wakasilele in the most humiliating way possible that he had committed a breach of good manners, his friend presented him with the most valuable asset he possessed —a pig. The emotion Wakasilele was struggling with was shame, and presumably contrition.[8]

The parable of the wicked husbandmen (Lk 29:9–19) is a story in similar vein, of a man whose ambassadors were spurned and whose authority was mocked. So he sent the closest thing to himself—his own son—in an attempt to appeal to the tenants' sense of shame, by allowing himself to be vulnerable; he put *himself* in the hands of his tenants, by giving his son. Of course he failed, but perhaps the parable reveals the motivation of the father who sent his son, not out of stupidity or ignorance, but rather in a vain but eloquent appeal to unwritten rules of honor.

Again, in spite of the "rules," extreme need may confer the right to receive. So even if a person has nothing to give, and if no one makes a gift, such a person may be entitled to "steal." And many societies institutionalize days of "carnival" in which a redistribution of goods and food takes place, or "role reversal," during which rich and poor, powerful and weak change places, and a "leveling out" process is experienced. West African boys stealing food from elders and British Army officers serving the ranks are not too far apart, from this perspective.

Where gifts are received and repaid almost immediately, there is probably a system in which the participants are of equal status, and the gift exchange does not bespeak a "power flow" or the deliberate creation and maintenance of relationships of indebtedness. But when the exchange is asymmetrical and the repayments delayed, there is likely to be a significant flow of power, and in this fashion: if a "big man" dispenses largesse and belittles his generosity, telling the recipients that he is in absolutely no hurry for a return, then clearly he is denying his short-term need; this is a statement of power. Other people are in his debt, and his relationship is one of superiority over the others. For their part, they remain "indebted" so long as the "gift" is not repaid. It may in fact never be repaid; but the "big man" remains "big" by virtue of unclaimed debts. He is the "rich almoner" who "wounds" others by his "charity."

In those cases where the recipient *does not want or feel the need to repay* immediately, there is freedom-in-indebtedness. When the recipient *cannot repay* immediately, there is servitude. And it makes no difference whether the "donor" says that repayment does not matter; this is a question of pride and reciprocity, and it certainly *does* matter both to the recipient and to the nature of the relationship. To the westerner who may feel that gifts are "free," such attitudes will seem incomprehensible or petty; to the "insider" things are not so simple, and a non-reciprocal gift, an unreciprocated gift, and a simple once-only gift are unfamiliar and "immoral" notions.

Kula Rings, Potlatching, and Mumis

Quite briefly, let me illustrate some of the complexities of gift exchange, as well as some of the satisfaction to be gained from successful puzzle-solving, by surveying three widely scattered and classic cases.

THE KULA AND THE KULA RING

One of the best known instances of gift exchange and ceremonial reciprocity—and one which I simplify here—is an institution which involves many of the adult men of several islands, some up to three hundred miles apart, between New Guinea to the west and the Solomon Islands to the east, in the Melanesian part of the Pacific.[9]

After elaborate preparations that take months, if not years, canoes are built and ritually prepared, and an expedition sets off to a specific island, taking all kinds of objects of trade. But this is not a trading expedition. The seafarers are going to *receive* either red-shell necklaces or white-shell armbands, depending upon their relationship to their partner on the other island, and on the affinity between particular islands within the context of a much wider system. It is not that the necklaces and armbands are not easily made or in plentiful supply; the red and white shell is itself neither scarce nor difficult to fashion. But these objects—*kula* valuables, collectively known as *vaygu'a*, are the most prized possessions of the recipients. And that is not all; they are not to be "possessed" or "owned" for long, but must be given away quite soon after they are received.

Several island communities have created a "*kula* exchange ring." The necklaces are given away by one partner to one of his other partners, but only according to an established pattern, and only in a clockwise direction from one island to the other. Concurrently, but in a counter-clockwise direction, go the armbands. So there are many expeditions and an ongoing interchange in which articles pass from one person to another in opposite directions. And expeditions are mounted from one island to another, according to the "rules" of the "*kula* ring," in which those who receive the visitors give the gifts, and those who go on expedition receive the gifts.

Each member of a pair of partners gives one kind of object and receives the other (but not in direct exchange, for this is "delayed" and "indirect" exchange, in which large spans of time and many different partners are involved) according to a formal pattern of ceremonial. Yet this is no mere formalism; competition is fierce. There are certain specially prized armbands and necklaces that have long and well-known histories. A person who eventually receives one is lionized by his fellows, even though he must give it away before long. But he will have several other similar objects, and he can exercise choice as he disperses these among his other partners, bestowing the prized ones on special partners, or clinging to a favored one for as long as possible. But the way of the *kula* is for the "giver" to *appear* to disparage his gift, to seem to be unattached to it and uncaring about giving it away. Then others will be impressed by his "detachment" and his prestige will rise. There is no room here for the "miser" who hoards the best necklaces or armbands. The whole point of this *kula* exchange is to keep the flow of "goods-in-circulation" and not to staunch the flow by holding on to things for too long. Partnership demands interaction through gift exchange, and a person who shows no largesse will soon be receiving only second and third rate *kula* goods, eventually forcing him out of this elaborate and ostentatious interaction.

The "rules" of *kula* exchange, and the context in which it is operative, are much more impressive than this outline. The general code of etiquette that governs behavior is quite rigid. A presentation gift is "de rigueur," and as the expedition leaves, a counter-gift is made, which must be at least equal in value to the opening gift. And this is before the real *kula* exchange gets under way. There is absolutely no haggling or bargaining at any stage—this is a far cry from barter, and explicitly creates indebtedness.

But even with the merest outline, I think it is possible to illustrate some of our original points: that gift exchange can be ongoing, elaborate, morally binding and quite different from economic exchange; that reciprocity is characteristic of gift exchange; that the actual gift is not as important as the symbolic exchange or "total prestation," which is the communication of and between people; that strict "rules" and expectations may be perfectly compatible with the development of interpersonal relationships; that reciprocal relationships can develop between peers, but once they become asymmetrical, the peer relationship is threatened; that the maintenance of gift exchange relationships presupposes "relevance," and when one party deems the relationship irrelevant (for a variety of reasons) then it will atrophy; and that "gifts" may become "poison" if one does not work at relationship or if one party's self-interest begins to dominate.

So much for the *kula,* an elaborately encoded and contextualized system of gift exchange and symbolic exchange. If I have left many unanswered questions, that is at least partly deliberate; people who are left with serious questions about the moral implications of gift exchange for missionaries are probably beginning to perceive the "system" underlying the behavior. It is not random activity, but something that warrants further exploration. So the more unanswered questions there are, the more effective may have been this section.

THE POTLATCH OF NORTH AMERICA

Along the west coast of the North American continent, from Vancouver to Alaska, in native American societies such as the Haida, the Tlingit, the Kwakiutl, the Nootka and the Bella Coola, the institution of the potlatch was practiced in various forms. But rather than trying to explain it first, let me start from the opposite end, that of manifest behavior rather than underlying belief.

It is sometimes claimed that the Hudson's Bay Company *really* made its fortune by selling blankets to the native Americans on the coast, and that they in turn threw thousands upon thousands of these blankets into the Pacific before looking round to replenish their stocks! These statements certainly do contain some truth, as do reports that people engaged in orgies of destruction in which they beggared themselves and their families. Potlatching was since declared illegal—not to any great effect, not with convincing authority, and latterly only nominally at best—in the United States and Canada, though it is by no means dead. So what is it all about?

"Potlatch"—which is now in the English dictionary—comes from a Nootka word meaning "gift" or, probably more accurately, "the act of giving," though we need to recall the distinction between simple gifts familiar to us, and "gift" in the present context. There are recorded cases of communities stacking up thousands—ten, twenty, thirty thousand—of Hudson's Bay Blankets and then watching them sink or sail away as they threw them into the ocean. Potlatches are [were] forms of institutionalized behavior, and occur as markers of life-crises or at times of status-change. Some of the most common were the house-building potlatch, the vengeance potlatch, the face-saving potlatch and the funeral potlatch, and we will look at a couple of these.[10]

The Haida couple who want to be taken seriously will prepare for a decade or more for a house-building potlatch. When they feel they have made all the necessary arrangements, they will invite friends and neighbors, and together work as a team throughout the winter months to obtain wood and other materials for their new house and totem pole. Such work is long and exhausting, but the winter months are enlivened by partying and feasting—at the expense of the hosts. But costly though this may be, it is not yet a potlatch. Only at the conclusion of house building does the wife (this is a matrilineal society) throw a potlatch. On the appointed day all those who have helped in some way will gather and be seated according to rank. And the wife then proceeds to lavish gifts of household goods, utensils, fur coats and (inevitably!) blankets on one and all. The closure is signaled when she gives her husband an old and torn blanket or token, which says that there is nothing left. All is finished, and in return for their new house and totem pole, the couple have impoverished themselves before their friends; everyone is happy. The couple now have a house and friends who are disposed to help them; the "exploited" friends have some resources to help them in their own potlatch, and have extended their fellowship and interdependence.

The vengeance potlatch is a rather different affair. Somewhat like Wakasilele (whom we met earlier), an insulted man will go to the person who insulted him and begin to destroy his own property. He does not destroy what he does not really need, but deliberately ruins or breaks up or casts away what is most dear to him. The adversary is *morally obliged* to follow suit and to outdo the insulted person, or else he loses respect and status and ends up disgraced. Vengeance potlatches may have been involved when Hudson's Bay Company blankets were so profligately destroyed. But this is no wanton vandalism; it is a matter of honor and social standing.

Potlatches may also be in the form of gargantuan feasts given by chiefs competing for support and social ascendancy. By deliberately beggaring oneself and gaining status, one is ensuring that everyone else is a short-term beneficiary, though in the long term such beneficiaries are indebted to the chief in some way. And when a challenger to highest status has finished his ostentatious display of wealth in use, the incumbent chief is forced to try to outdo the splendor of his rival, in order to maintain his position. Failure to do so means loss of position; success in doing so ensures the flow of goods and services throughout the community, rather than their staunching and accumulation in the hands of the chief.

Contrast these attitudes to wealth, relationships, gift exchange and prestige, with attitudes current in other societies where people want to accumulate rather than redistribute, where interrelationship and indebtedness are considered *a bad thing*, and where the rich get richer and the poor get poorer. More characteristic of such other (capitalist) societies, it is precisely as the rich get richer and less reciprocally related to other people that they are somehow accorded increased status and fame, though they may have done nothing to benefit the society as a whole.

Potlatching illustrates the obligation of giving, receiving and returning. Unless one gives, one remains a nonentity." It is a matter of responsibility and honor to accept an invitation to a potlatch. And, having accepted, one is indebted, and this new relationship carries its own obligations. Actual repayment is not always made, for the bountiful benefactor may not "call in" or redeem all that has been given away; but a person does remain in a morally inferior position unless and until there has been a reciprocal gesture. Refusal to accept potlatch gifts is also possible, but this is an admission of inability or unwillingness to enter into relationship, and is judged accordingly. But overall, the potlatch illustrates that people can and should be interdependent and not independent, and that wealth is nothing unless it is being used.

THE "MUMI" OF THE SOLOMON ISLANDS

Returning almost to the Trobriands of the *kula* exchange, we stop off at Bougainville island, where the Siuai people call their "big man" a *mumi*. It seems that it is every young man's ambition to become a *mumi*, and those who pursue this goal seriously will work diligently and with great self-abnegation. If a young man thus succeeds in persuading his wife, relatives and friends of his determination, they help him prepare a feast. Thus is the number of his "supporters" increased, and he sets about building, with all the help as he can muster, a clubhouse or longhouse in which his friends can relax and eat. If his hospitality is really impressive—and this will demand that he spend all his waking hours trying to please—people will start to refer to him as a *mumi*. Now those who are providing labor and resources for the *mumi* will expect some acknowledgment or recompense, but may well be satisfied inasmuch as they bask in his reflected glory and are known as his intimates; but the *mumi* has no easy job maintaining his status.[12]

Sooner or later, an aspiring *mumi* will feel ready to challenge for the position of preeminence—or will have retired, just as political hopefuls in a democracy withdraw from the race—at a special feast. Rather like the chief who throws a potlatch, the aspiring *mumi* will throw an enormous party, at which a record of all the food—pigs, coconuts, sago—and drink is kept. Everyone is invited and everyone benefits. And the incumbent *mumi* must reciprocate with an even more lavish feast within the year. Failure to do so reduces him to the ranks, and the cycle burgeons again.

The point to underscore here is not simply that there is rule-governed behavior operating, but that here we see another system for *redistribution;* and that it is precisely in the "communism" or "leveling out" that the human aspirations to status differences can flourish. What often happens in contemporary "capitalist-mentality" countries *at the expense of* the people in general is effected *to the benefit of* people in general, in other societies. Not that everything is perfect; far from it. But there *are* other viable ways of relating and living in society.

A *mumi* consciously undertakes a life of competition and risk, and sometimes fails in his ambition. But his struggles and pretentions do provide entertainment, diversion and conversation for many; and though it may be true that many benefit marginally, rather than few substantially, it is also true that few risk ruin if he fails, though many might be slightly incommoded; and, further, the more competing *mumi* there are, the more goods and food there will be in circulation. But even the most successful *mumi*, granted he has gained enormous prestige, is not immune from all strife; the *mumi* is not in a position to force others to conform to his wishes, and quite often is required to live very modestly in order to meet his obligations to his followers. As the saying goes: "The giver of the feast takes the bones and the stale cake; the meat and the fat go to the others."

Before colonial policy outlawed it, controlled warfare was a constituent part of the life of at least some of the *mumi,* and a way of their obtaining resources. Several warrior *mumi* would fight as allies or antagonists in such a way that there developed an incipient political system of segmentary opposition and alliance. But even here there was a significant element of interdependence and responsibility, for the *mumi* was personally responsible for each of those he took to war; "insurance" had to be paid to the kin of any person killed, and the *mumi* was also responsible for providing a fitting funeral—sufficient obligation to give pause to the more headstrong *mumi*.[13]

GENERAL LESSONS AND FURTHER ISSUES

Once again we note that reciprocity takes many forms, and that what may be called "redistributor chiefs" may be an intrinsic part of the vitality of a society. But if we simply look at surface behavior without any understanding of the rationale as developed from within the group, we will fail to appreciate what is really happening, and perhaps more importantly we will be unable to discover a reasonable and relevant point of entry, for ourselves and for the gospel. And we now have enough material, from the *kula,* the potlatch and the *mumi* contexts, to move to a discussion of specifically mission-related issues.

But, first, a few questions might be appropriate for us to ponder. Can we appreciate the force of a system of gift exchange that is both rule-governed and spontaneous, and a matter of both personal initiative and mutuality? What is the significance of the respect which people show for wealth *in use,* and how might our own attitudes toward stewardship and toward savings —"unearned income"?—be challenged and perhaps reassessed? Apart from the obvious differences, what similarities and parallels can be found between our own experience and the mechanics of potlatch? Does potlatch or *kula* or the behavior of the *mumi* embody certain "gospel values" of which perhaps we have been unaware, values that we can search for in more familiar social institutions henceforth? And why, when we "haggle" in distant marketplaces, do we hold so tenaciously to the idea of "bargain" or "fair price," fearing that we will be exploited by the seller who makes different prices for different people? Can we perhaps now see how inappropriate such narrowly "economic" behavior is?[14]

The Missionary, the Gift, and the Gospel

If it is legitimate to view the world as a set of puzzles, and to declare that the minister on the edge of familiar cultures or living in unfamiliar ones must grapple with and try to solve many of them, then what can we say about the institution of gift exchange and the systems that underlie it from culture to culture? We could of course reduce the problem to a very narrowly focused area—the particular field in which we personally are working at a given time—and try to address it that way. But here I have chosen to expand rather than to contract our focus, because it seems to me that we can benefit from some generalizations and some overarching patterns, as well as from specific conclusions.

I think of gift exchange as a universal metaphor—perhaps a "root paradigm"—in human society. By discovering its manifestations in a given community, we may go a significant way to understanding the "language" of human interaction and reciprocity. Without such an understanding we may well fail utterly to make sense of anything other than isolated cases, and even they cannot be fully revealed unless situated in a broad context. How can we understand marriage, ownership, the status of the person, or amity and warfare, much less teach the eucharist[15] or matrimony, confirmation or baptism itself, without a real familiarity with a "root paradigm" such as this?[16] *This* is precisely the kind of root on to which the gospel might be grafted—and if we fail to find such roots, then we might expect the gospel itself to fail to take root.

The problems relating to adequate evangelization and authentic inculturation or contextualization of the gospel are legion. But some at least can be tackled with real hope of success. The first thing to look at is the attitude, or more correctly the package of attitudes, which a missionary brings to a culture, a people. It is clearly impossible and ultimately undesirable—because a real challenge, such as the challenge of the gospel, has to have the force of novelty, unfamiliarity, and real difficulty, since it calls to conversion, and such a catalyst is essentially an external agent—for the missionary to be totally accommodating and open-minded; socialization processes have formed us and provided points of reference and anchors in the bed of reality. And since there are many worlds and many realities, we must accept the necessity of learning anew. Yet before we can do that, we must accept ourselves and try to acknowledge our starting points and perspectives.

For communication with another—another person with another perspective in another reality in another world—there must be mutual intelligibility, not only in linguistic terms but in terms of attitudes and behavior, values and beliefs. And it is here that the missionary typically meets frustration. But it is equally necessary to acknowledge that the people who were living and relating before missionaries arrived also experience frustration, tension and incomprehension when the latter appear on the scene. It is at this point that gift exchange can become a language, often more effective than mere linguistic dexterity; but sadly the reality can be that attitudes are set, and mutual unintelligibility marks and mars relationships, when neither the missionaries nor the hosts adequately understand the message which the other wishes to convey.

By looking at the psychology and sociology of gift exchange against specific backgrounds of culturally determined meanings, and with a view to contextualizing not simply a theology but a praxis of Christian living, I think we can tease out significant implications for mission.

The Obligation To Give

We missionaries do not doubt this; we are professional "givers" who are accustomed to spending our lives refining our altruism and lavishing care on others. But others too experience the same obligation and the same need to give. How much do we acknowledge their rights in this regard, and how much do we allow for and encourage their giving, *on their terms?* We give on our terms, and sometimes we can allow others to give, but also on our terms. Where is the reciprocity here? Do we know anything about the terms and the ways in which other people may want or feel obligated to give to us? Do we not demean others when we inhibit their customary patterns of giving, thus making ourselves appear aloof and quite unmarked by indebtedness? If indebtedness is a hallmark of gift exchange—and thus of humanness itself—how are we perceived by our hosts, as bearers of this hallmark? In our concern for all we "do" for others, are we perhaps insensitive to what the others (try to or might like to) do for us? Are we guilty of being the "rich almoners" whom Mauss so decried, and who so humiliate and antagonize the recipients of their "charity"?

The Obligation To Receive

We have seen by now that giving is *not* the prerogative or duty of one party while receiving is proper only to the other; both giving and receiving characterize each party in an ongoing interrelationship. Are we, then, as attentive to our social duty as receivers as we are to our perceived moral obligation as givers? There is just as much of a moral obligation to be a receiver as there is to be a giver—perhaps more, since to receive is to allow the giver the initiative, and it empowers or liberates the giver for a relationship. Not to receive is to refuse to place ourselves—however temporarily—in an inferior position; yet without a temporary inferior, the relationship cannot move to one of reciprocity and mutuality, because no indebtedness has taken place.

But even if we *do* acknowledge our moral responsibility to be receivers as well as givers, there is still that tendency for us to be so *on our own terms,* and this we must continuously and firmly resist. Do we, perhaps, *demand* immediate return of what we have lent, or immediate reciprocation of what bounty we have extended, and then try to justify our attitude as one of "justice" or "good stewardship"? Do we emphasize the people's responsibility to give so that we can receive "upkeep" or feel entitled to "recompense" "for services rendered"? Do we concentrate on *money* as a sign of reciprocity, rather than on other things? As we saw, money is not easily situated within the context of gift exchange; it belongs more in the economic than in the moral sphere, but people seek relationships with us and not simply economic ties. And it may be much more appropriate for them to share the "fruits of the earth and work of human hands" than paper or coin! So how do we show—and persuade others of—our trust and acceptance, surely the basis of mutuality and essential ingredients of authentic mission? We really have to *learn* to be gracious receivers, and in so doing come to accept what may be tedious to accept—things we do not really want or appreciate, or for which we have no "need" or "use." Not only might this give us sympathy for others who have to accept the unsolicited gifts we press on them; it might teach us that there is more to life and to authentic, mutual relationships than our own intuitions or preferences allow for.

THE OBLIGATION TO REPAY

This, as we have seen, is the essence of enduring relationships. We missionaries, however, tarred with the brush of rational capitalist economic theory, may often think of repayment as the *conclusion* to a transaction or the *completion* of a contract. And as stewards and professionally honest people, we take seriously both the speed with which repayment is made and the obligation not to fall into debt too easily. If we are to communicate in local vernaculars, however, and if we are to make any headway in forming

Christian communities of people who expect and rely on interdependence, we will have to learn how to be considerably less independent and more obligated, how to repay honestly but not too hastily, and how to ensure that we are always bonded in some debt to some people, lest we cut the links with others and set ourselves adrift from the mainland, getting swept into the tidal bore where there are no relationships and everyone fights for survival. Our cult of efficiency and contractual obligations divorced from real human interaction does not endear us—and may make us incomprehensible and unreachable—to those into whose lives we have dropped; and our failure to learn the grammar of gift exchange will certainly make us less than relevant and less than warmly appreciated, and the message we bring less than comprehensible or acceptable.

Do we have any idea of the *resources* to which we have access, or of how easy it is for us to give people the impression that (in spite of what we say), we do not really need their efforts? Do we effectively belittle their attempts at reciprocity? How do we *repay* them; not simply how do we *give,* but how do we *respond* to them? Sometimes, under the guise of good stewardship, do we not pay them grudgingly and meanly, and is our style of repayment more a "contractual" style than a "relational" or "interpersonal" style? Are we simply acting as "economic man [woman]" when to act as "gift exchanger" would be much more to the point?

THE OBLIGATION TO LEARN AND TO CHANGE

Have we not always said that the gospel and the grace of God are free, unmerited gifts? Why have we been so slow to follow up the implications here? Free and unmerited they may be, but they are *gift*. And a gift must not only be given but received. And how can we determine whether a gift has been received? The Kreen Akrore left the gifts untouched or unaccepted; that was plain. In how many cultures have missionaries worked for years, to find their well-intentioned gifts untouched or unassimilated? What message is being conveyed here? Cannot missionaries read the message, or are they simply unable to accept it? And why might such gifts be unaccepted in the first place, bearing in mind the universal practice of gift exchange? Perhaps the gift seems meaningless, or inadequately contextualized, or useless, or inappropriate, or embarrassing. Missionaries know from personal experience what such gifts are like, so might not other people too have difficulty in understanding even the most well-meant gift, especially if its nature and purpose are not carefully clarified?

The responsibility rests with the donor, to make the gift acceptable and comprehensible. But there does come a point where the donor must acknowledge that, for whatever reason, the gift has not been accepted *in its present form.* What flexibility do missionaries have which would be compatible with their integrity? What integrity do they have if they refuse to allow a potential recipient to refuse? And what theological and evangelical freedom do they have to recognize the freedom of others to decline as well as to accept?[17]

I think I appreciate the motivations of missionaries, but it does also seem timely now to remark that our plans have often been set before we arrived, and our interaction has sometimes been anything but spontaneous and reciprocal. We have talked to people, but often talked *down.* We have listened to people, but often *selectively.* We have craved relationship with people, but often only as *givers.* We may well have set ourselves to learn from people, but primarily and paradoxically as their *teachers.*[18] We have brought a clear message to people, but often in the wrong *language.* Our language and our listening, our relationships and our teaching have been impregnated with power and the control of initiatives, with righteousness and certainty. The language and metaphor of gift exchange may still offer us a balance and show us the value of incompleteness and uncertainty, surrender of initiative and risk-taking, vulnerability and indebtedness.

Is it possible, then, to have and to present a theology that really takes other people seriously, really works toward their liberation from oppressive structures and metaphors, really roots with their roots and grows with their growth? Or must theology or catechesis degenerate and wither on the vine, producing only at best the bitter-sweet fruits of hierarchy and standardization, or a joyless crop of enslavement and inequality?

Have we tried, informally or systematically, to perceive "gospel-values" embedded in the behavior of people of other cultures? Or have we too easily assumed that there were none and that God had not reached the people before our arrival? And if we have been over-negative, could we not now find in the language and speech of gift exchange some clear echoes of the gospel?

QUESTIONS FOR THE ROAD

Once again, we conclude by looking at some possible questions: What does a study of gift exchange contribute to our knowledge of the message we carry as gift, and how might it challenge us to share that gift with others?

How do we give it? receive it? repay it? Are we now any more prepared to concede that "the gift is never free" means more than meets the eye, and contains deep pools from which we may draw wisdom for the apostolate? Do we notice how we hold on to power when we try to orchestrate patterns of giving and receiving, and fail to respond to local themes? Are we aware of the dangers of contractual/economic relationships where reciprocal/moral relationships should flourish? How do we go about discovering authentic spiritualities both for ourselves in other cultural worlds and for those more at home in such worlds? How can we have a spirituality *unless* it is rooted in the local culture with its sights and smells, its sounds and textures? And how could we hope to be incorporated in another culture other than through its own social forms and social institutions, of which gift exchange is such a characteristic one?

Thus far, have the kinds of issues we have raised brought us any closer to a culturally-sensitive proclamation of the good news, and what can we learn from a study of gift exchange and associated behavior which may facilitate or inhibit evangelization?

Here then is food for the journey and meditation for the road: some familiar scriptural references for study, discussion and prayer, in the light of this chapter:

"If anyone should press you into service for one mile, go with that person two miles. Give to whoever begs from you. Do not turn your back on the borrower" (Mt 5:41–42).

"The gift you received, give as gift" (Mt 10:8).

"A gift opens every door for you and wins you access to the great" (Prov 18:16).

"The generous person has many to court his favor; to the one who gives, everyone is friend" (Prov 19:6).

". . . divine grace through Jesus Christ came as *abundant free gift*" (Rom 5:15).

"Each one of you has received a special gift; so, like good stewards responsible for all these different graces of God, put yourselves at the service of others" (1 Pet 4:10).

"The amount you measure out is the amount you will be given" (Mk 4:24).

"Give and there will be gifts for you . . . good measure, pressed down, shaken together, running over" (Lk 6:38).

"God never takes back his gifts nor revokes his choice" (Rom 11:29).

Notes and Bibliography

1. Edmund Leach, in a very accessible and entertaining introduction to social anthropology, includes a chapter on our subject. See *Social Anthropology*, Glasgow, Fontana, 1982, Chapter 5, "Debt, Relationship, Power."

2. The classic work of Marcel Mauss is available in an English translation from the original French. See *The Gift*, London, Cohen and West, 1970.

3. Another entertaining and informative general survey of anthropology is by Ioan Lewis, *Social Anthropology in Perspective*, Harmondsworth, England, Penguin Books, 1976. Chapter 7 is entitled "Exchange and Market."

4. Bronislaw Malinowski's *Argonauts of the Western Pacific* is the *locus classicus* for *kula*. The book, originally published in 1922, is available from New York, Dutton & Co. Inc., 1961.

5. A rather unusual and very interesting book is Margaret Hebblethwaite's *Motherhood and God*, London, Geoffrey Chapman, 1984. In her Chapter 10, "Understanding and Support," she tackles the issue of the assistance that mothers need during child-rearing. But the help must not become suffocating or smack too much of "charity"; otherwise the mother begins to lose her sense of individuality and integrity. Sometimes, therefore, it is *necessary* for a mother to have a simple "contractual" arrangement with a baby-sitter, rather than to be continuously indebted and unable to repay well-intentioned relatives—a well-taken point.

Anne Wilson Schaef takes up a very similar issue, that of *co-dependency*, in which an individual is unable to escape the role of supporter or nurturer to a person in an addictive situation. Perhaps as missionaries some of us are "addicted" to our roles—and the status attached—as "providers," and the people we ostensibly serve become dependent upon us rather than independent or truly interdependent. In such situations, a missionary cannot escape a relationship in which he or she is a "giver" while local people are unable to free themselves from the role of "receiver." See her *Co-Dependence, Misunderstood, Mistreated*, San Francisco, Harper and Row, 1986, and *When Society Becomes an Addict*, San Francisco, Harper and Row, 1987.

6. If we understand "repayment" as that which brings "closure" to a "transaction," then the better term here might be "return." "Return" here would indicate that the relationships continue into a new phase.

7. A recent article reappraised the perspective of Marcel Mauss, distinguishing it from that of Malinowski and blaming the translator of the English edition of *The Gift* for misrepresenting Mauss. I have drawn on the work of Jonathan Parry and his article "*The Gift,* the Indian Gift, and the 'Indian Gift,' " in *Man,* 21 (3) 1986:453–473.

8. Michael Young gives this example in his *Fighting With Food,* Cambridge, England, Cambridge University Press, 1971, p. xix.

9. Apart from Malinowski, many others have researched the *kula* or drawn from the master's work. Some accessible references include Ioan Lewis, *Social Anthropology in Perspective,* 199–203, and Edmund Leach, *Social Anthropology,* 155ff (references already quoted).

10. Ronald and Evelyn Rohner were the authors of *The Kwakiutl: Indians of British Columbia,* New York, Holt, Rinehart and Winston, 1970; also Stuart Piddocke, "The Potlatch System of the Southern Kwakiutl: A New Perspective," in Andrew P. Vayda (ed.), *Environment and Cultural Behavior,* Garden City, N.J.: Natural History Press, 1969:130–156. But perhaps the easiest reference is to be found in the *Encyclopaedia Britannica.*

11. This statement needs to be qualified. A person who aspired to higher status through potlatching would indeed remain a nonentity by refusing to give lavishly; but not everyone entertains such aspirations. Invitations would not be extended indiscriminately, but only to and by those in competition.

12. The ethnographer of the Siuai was Douglas Oliver, and his book is *A Solomon Island Society: Kinship and Leadership Among the Siuai of Bougainville,* Cambridge, Harvard University Press, 1955.

13. In his *Cannibals and Kings,* Glasgow, Fontana, 1977:80–83, Marvin Harris deals with the *mumi.*

14. It *is* of course economic, but *not only* economic behavior.

15. See the article by Andre Fossion in *Lumen Vitae,* 1980:409–416, "The Eucharist as an Act of Exchange."

16. Victor Turner spoke of "root paradigms" on several occasions. I think the usage varies somewhat, and classically Turner used to refer to one's self-actualization through the exercise of a fundamental option. However, the use of the word "paradigm" is much broader of course, indicating a model or pattern. I use "root paradigm" here, tentatively, to indicate *a very deeply rooted, perhaps super-cultural form of behavior.*

17. Vincent Donovan looks at this, among many other issues, in that thought-provoking and disturbing book which has already been recommended, *Christianity Rediscovered.*

18. I am certainly not opposed to teachers or to teaching! It is, of course, attitudes that would equate teaching with indoctrination rather than with reciprocity and education that are very dangerous indeed.

Five

The Missionary as Stranger

As members of alien cultures, missionaries can hardly expect to become assimilated by the host populations. Yet without at least some level of inculturation there can be no communication of aspirations and values. So how might we deal with paradox and marginality?

Introduction

CHALLENGE AND PARADOX

If communities of believers are to grow in response to grace, they must be true to themselves: their liturgies, their ecclesial disciplines, their customs and the rest, must glorify God in ways that reflect the wonders of creation through the windows of their experience and in the light of their culture. And their faith must enrich their lives. Thus, a Central African community must necessarily embody their Christianity differently from a Caribbean or an Amazonian, an Indonesian or a European community. Diversity is as characteristic of human society as it is authentic as an expression of religion.

When the word of God passes from one recipient to another, it passes through linguistic, historical, temporal and cultural "filters." The Christian who transmits the message must do so as carefully and as loyally as possible, while also acknowledging that all truth does not reside in the particular *form* in which it is held (the good news does not come *only* in English, or *only* in the King James Version or the New American Bible translation). The message is, to some degree, free of any one specific form or any one particular messenger, though of course it must be encoded and transmitted if it is to communicate. And in its reception, it is transmuted, internalized, absorbed. Not only the integrity of the content and the meaning of the message but also its diversity of form are central to the gospel and the process of evangelization. Here is the challenge!

And so to the paradox. We missionaries are impelled in a centrifugal direction, *away from* our familiar world. But we are thereby drawn centripetally, *toward* the world of others, a world that existed before us and independently of our knowledge and consent. In going "away from" and "toward," we move only as far as the margins, both of our own world and that of others. We cannot completely leave our own world of meanings and values; we never break out into "space." But neither can we become situated at the very center of another world; that would be rude and arrogant to presume, and impossible to effect: we are simply not that significant.

The paradox, therefore, lies partly in the fact that we must allow other people to receive the message we transmit, but according to their own capacity and integrity; yet we must carefully hand on the tradition which has interpreted it through the centuries. And partly it lies in the fact that we who come in the name of the Lord must prepare to be evangelized by the people and converted by the Spirit; much as we want to be accessible and relevant we are perforce only marginal to their culture and must resist all temptations to colonize or patronize, yet genuinely wish to establish communities of faith with them.

PROCEDURE

The subject matter of this final chapter warrants a modification in our approach. As before, there will be bibliographical references; but we will look more directly at the biblical resources, and the chapter itself will be offered as a basis for reflection and meditation. This chapter will make more direct appeal to our spirituality as missionaries. My intention is to conclude by focusing on the status of Jesus in relation to others as a model for our own ministry.

"FOREIGN" AND "STRANGE"

It is not comfortable to feel "foreign" or "strange," so many of us wriggle or fidget as we resist the discomfort. Or perhaps we minimize movement that would put us in the position of outsiders; and if movement is unavoidable, we seek out a familiar face. This may be our pattern, whether walking into a room full of "strangers" in our own society, traveling overseas on vacation, or undertaking a significant journey into another cultural or language group. And when we do find ourselves outnumbered, wherever we are, we tend to regard the others, not ourselves, as the strangers! So what in fact constitutes a stranger? Who are strangers? How do we personally understand the term? And could we ever easily accept that we ourselves might be as strange as the strangers we see around us? This is the perspective that beckons us: it is we ourselves, not others, who are the strangers.

It could be said that some people—and missionaries will number significantly among them—actually seem to enjoy going into unfamiliar situations. Yet I believe it is equally true to argue that to some degree every one of us tries to manipulate and control an unfamiliar situation; and, moreover, some missionaries, public profession to the contrary, are xenophobic or even racist. This is nothing new; we are all aware of these things, at least dimly. But to deny our limitations and tendencies is to resist grace. This chapter may help us uncover some attitudes that need redeeming.

The dictionary may be a refuge for tired minds, but it is undoubtedly an Aladdin's cave of treasures. Under the entries for "foreign" we find words like "not pertinent," "abnormal," "alien," and "strange." Turning to the entry for "strange," we note "peculiar," "odd," "extraordinary." And under "stranger" we stumble on "a person not easily explained," "an unfamiliar person," and "any person one does not know"; entries also include "a guest or visitor." We might ponder here on how well- or ill-fitting we feel these terms are, *as applied to ourselves.* Can we acknowledge that *we are* "not pertinent," "abnormal," or "not easily explained"? We are certainly familiar with fixing these labels on others; how easily can we now remove the tags and apply them to our own personas and persons? However else we appear to others, we most certainly are—by definition—strange.

Only when we assimilate the fact of our strangeness—with whatever that may imply in a particular culture or situation—will we be able to glimpse the impression that our behavior and our preaching might have. But if we have never been really vulnerable before other people, if we have always found refuge in the security of a group of like-minded missionaries who preceded us and blazed our trail, if we have been meticulously socialized to think of our values and attitudes as normative for and demanded of others, and if we have never prayed for the gift that Robert Burns immortalized, the gift to see ourselves as others see us, then I fear we will be unable to minister as Jesus ministered.

DEFINITIONS AND BOUNDARIES

People stake out their turf and beat the bounds of their domains' and thereby position themselves and each other in the world. They thus delimit or define their space and whatever occupies it. A definition is (by definition!) a boundary, and as such it may mark not only the physical world but the moral dimensions of virtues like truth or beauty, duty or right. People who have no sense of the limits to safety or to pain, or of the difference between friend or foe, might appear very courageous and open-minded in the short term, but in the longer term will cease to exist! Consequently societies that have survived will have developed attitudes to their boundaries and what lies beyond. People beyond the boundaries or beyond the pale² are called foreigners and treated as strangers. Thus does the human species remake the world.

Because no two societies live in precisely the same relationship to the environment and to their neighbors, no two societies will "define" their world in exactly the same way. But all of us will learn, and effectively take for granted, to treat *our* definitions as true, *our* reality as "really real." This is not problematic until we step to the threshold of another world where our definitions come under threat and our reality is seen as idiosyncrasy.

It is *normal* to joke about and perhaps belittle the definitions or reality of others, as retailed by travelers returning from distant worlds. It could sometimes be a healthy attitude, inasmuch as it draws us back to the structures on which are built our own world-of-meaning. But when we leave the comfort of our world and walk into the world of others, then it is no joke; and if we fail to extend the courtesy of taking other people seriously, then it is a decidedly unhealthy attitude.

What, then, should we do? To compromise our own points of reference is to abandon compass and walk on quicksand; however trusting it may appear, it is extremely risky and perhaps foolish. But to hold to our compass and footwear, when the compass swings widely and swimming is a more appropriate form of locomotion, is as stupid as it is conceited. If our sense of mission is so attached, either to the feckless or to the individualistic approach, then it is not surprising that we face confusion or opposition; and if that is where our treasure and our heart is, then our sense of mission is not at all that of Jesus.

If we find ourselves somewhat confused, we are not alone. No society can afford to be completely open to another, in terms either of welcome or of expectations; strangers are people who do not belong to the group and therefore do not share its history, its values, and its sanctions. People who have been insufficiently critical of strangers have sometimes not lived to tell the tale: there are no longer any indigenous Uruguayans or Tasmanians; and for every forty Brazilian Indians before the arrival of the Europeans, thirty-nine have been exterminated (from 1.2 million to 30,000)! The story of native American Indians in what is now the United States is largely the story of people outflanked and crushed by strangers or poisoned by their gifts. Trusting strangers can indeed be dangerous to health and life! So the idea that Christians should be welcomers of strangers (Mt 25:35–45) is as challenging as it is attractive. And any missionary who assumes that he or she should be welcomed with open arms is rather naive, or fails to appreciate the amount of trust this entails. It is one thing to want to show hospitality to the stranger; quite another thing is it to cede one's initiative and expectations. So if missionaries were more willing to allow *themselves* to be contextualized as *strangers,* rather than trying to position themselves as controllers, dictators, initiative-takers or proselytizers, then perhaps mutual relationships would be more conducive to a responsible and creative sharing of stories—and thus authentic evangelization—than has so often been the case.

Just as there is no true giver without a recipient, so there is no stranger in isolation; a stranger is, curiously, a social category. Normally, there can only be a stranger where there is a host. For missionaries to act as if there were no complementarity involved would be for us to demean relationships and make ourselves appear as "not pertinent," "abnormal," "peculiar" and "alien." And thus to understand the potential of a stranger for mutuality, change, and creativity, we must first examine the position of a host.

The Host

THE RIGHTS OF HOSTS

If we were to consider "the stranger" in an abstract sense, we would find that by implication our starting point is not actually the person "out there" but rather ourselves, or at least the person who makes another person a stranger: the non-stranger. In other words, the stranger is usually *someone else;* we do not normally define ourselves as strangers, much less "strange," because normally we are within our own familiar world, comfortable with ourselves and with our idiosyncrasies. But when we wander into an unfamiliar "world-of-meaning," then *the other,* occupying a comfortable vantage point in a familiar world-of-meaning, labels *us* as stranger.

Since the stranger is defined by the non-stranger, and since it is the latter who is at home, then the non-stranger (let us now say the "host") holds the initiative. Consequently the stranger—as one in need of food and lodging and hospitality—is already in debt to the host. It is entirely appropriate, not to say necessary, that the stranger feel unsure, ill-at-ease, vulnerable. It is of the very nature of strangers that they should experience such initial feelings, in order for the host to assume the attitudes appropriate to a host. To feel thus is testimony to the power of boundaries and definitions, since we feel "out of place" and "dislocated," which indeed we are. Again, thinking of the numerous cases of over-trusting hosts' being taken advantage of by unscrupulous strangers, the host really must try to retain the initiative and dictate the rules of encounter.

If the stranger does accept the position of deference and courtesy, allowing the hosts to be in control, then the interaction may begin on a basis of shared assumptions. The stranger is the intruder-in-need, and thus subordinate; the host is not, and thus superordinate. Only if each party accepts the appropriate role and its implications might relationships be established in time.

The Duties of Hosts

If we happen not to be used to being strangers, or, more problematical, if we do not wish to be dependent or vulnerable, the interaction will already feel stifling and unacceptable. Perhaps we resist the idea of putting ourselves in the hands of another; perhaps we sense that we might be exploited. And sadly this is indeed a feature of the individualism and self-sufficiency to which we are heirs. Sadly, too, it misses an essential point about the host in relation to the stranger. For, granted that the host does not want to risk extermination by hostile strangers—hence the need to "disarm" the stranger, both literally and figuratively—nevertheless there is built into cultures an element of hospitality to strangers that is by no means exploitative, and helps manifest the very humanity and sophistication that any host would wish to demonstrate. It is as if, in spite of the risks, the human species wants to make friends. And the best way I know how to express this is to examine the language of strangers.

English has the word "stranger," and another, quite different-looking word, "guest"; these words denote two separate categories. Maybe we think of a "stranger" as someone with little or no real identity, certainly not a friend; but a "guest" is much more familiar, someone we know and entertain freely. Perhaps we categorize strangers differently from guests, and treat them accordingly; but in many languages, the word for stranger *is* the word for guest, and there are not two different words. A stranger, therefore, is to be treated as a guest is to be treated. And a guest is thus, not simply a person one knows—partly because in a small world, or a village-based society, one knows everyone—but someone who, though not known, is nevertheless worthy of special treatment!

To say that a stranger is to be treated as a guest, and vice versa, is both to elevate the status of a stranger far beyond our own expectations and to draw our attention once more to the presence of "gospel-values" in cultures whose history was not influenced directly by the gospel. But the *rules* (unwritten, of course, and perhaps unstated) of hospitality are of great importance, and substantial responsibility is incumbent on the host. For just as it takes a host to make a stranger, so it takes a host to make a guest; but the host—the "non-stranger," the "non-guest"—though holding the initiative in the interaction, is also dependent on the other, because it also takes a guest to make a host!

THE EXPECTATIONS OF HOSTS

As we missionaries move in, and out of, other people's worlds, we should ask ourselves a number of questions: Do we show adequate and genuine deference to our hosts? Do we willingly acknowledge their authority in the situation, and their rights and duties as hosts? Do we allow ourselves to be adequately positioned as strangers, according to the legitimate needs of the hosts? Or do we try to seize initiatives, show them clearly what our expectations are, make demands on them, and thus effectively refuse the role of stranger, thereby impeding them from being adequate hosts? For no matter how well we rationalize our behavior—in terms of our virtuous independence, our respectful self-sufficiency, our ostentatious humility and our naive not-wanting-to-impose—if we fail to allow the other to be host we not only give offense and show great disrespect, but we sow seeds of confusion wherever we pass.

It is not that being strangers is easy, but being strangers is *necessary* if we are ultimately to cross any boundaries and discover any new relationships. To be a stranger willingly is to respect the rules of the game and allow the hosts the common courtesy of moving us from one category to another. Anything less and we pose a threat, or at least fail to make any sense to our hosts. And sometimes missionaries have not only ridden roughshod over people's sensibilities, but then reined in, turned round, and criticized them for not fulfilling expectations! So if we have a little more simplicity, not to say manners, perhaps we will allow ourselves to be received—according to the customs, and within the world-of-meaning of our hosts—as guests; and we will learn how to behave rather than jump to the unwarranted conclusion that other people do not. But it may already be too late; people have only so much tolerance, and unless strangers conform to certain expectations, they may no longer be welcomed, for self-preservation does come in here; so perhaps the damage has already been done. And if these seem strong words, we might bear in mind that missionaries have been seen time and time again to pay little or no attention to the *felt needs* of the hosts, to be arrogant and disrespectful, independent and unpredictable, and then to have made exorbitant demands on the people who were trying to extend tolerant hospitality.

THE AMBIVALENCE OF HOSTS

There is always likely to be some apprehension of strangers, since, after all, they are not like ourselves, not always consistent, not quite comprehensible! For this reason, expectations of and behavior toward strangers tend to be rather formal and somewhat stilted, as the host tries to get the measure of the outsiders. A feature of such interaction is that it is marked by ambivalence; after all, though the strangers are unknown, they probably bring gifts and have access to resources, yet still their motives are hidden and they may be power-full people.[3] Such ambivalence is a healthy and integral part of the host's attitude of self-preservation as well as of the cultivation of allies generally; in the course of time it will dissolve into acceptance if it does not harden into rejection.

And here again we missionaries are given pause. We may well be used to being "homecomers"—returning to familiar loved ones who will welcome us back warmly and treat us without ambivalence and with unconditional acceptance—but this is by no means the same as to arrive as strangers; to expect to be treated in a way appropriate to one context (homecoming), when the actual context is quite different, is unrealistic and unfair.[4] We have to be prepared to be strangers—to go into unfamiliar places among unfamiliar people—and to be welcomed with formality rather than unbounded warmth; that is the price of hospitality, which is itself the very basis of relationship. Without relationship there will be no chance of communities-of-faith. Without trust there will be no relationship. Without hospitality there will be no trust. And unless we approach as strangers, there will be no hospitality; for hospitality *means* the welcome appropriate for a host to extend to a stranger.

The Stranger

INTRODUCTION

In the 1870s, Holy Ghost missionaries were planning to open a mission in Bonthe, an island off the coast of Sierra Leone, West Africa. From time to time a French priest dressed in the long soutane or cassock—bearded, gaunt, senior, serious—traveled down to discuss possibilities. On one occasion he took with him a newly arrived priest, I believe, wearing a newer and more impressive soutane—clean-shaven, well-fed, young, amiable—who followed the older priest and kept quiet. A century later, going through some records and diaries of the time, I found that the local people had been very happy to greet the priest "and his wife!" To the local people who knew nothing about priests and little about white people, "beardless and with a 'dress' " presumably indicated "woman," while "walking behind a big man, and keeping quiet" was a sure sign of "wife." The strangers were effectively being contextualized or defined according to the available categories!

To allow ourselves to become a stranger effectively and with dignity, we must not only undertake a learning process, but also submit to some discomfort or worse. Failure to learn and defer will mark us as intransigent and ill-mannered, and thus not trustworthy; and yet too easy accommodation to the requirements of the hosts may mark us as weak and indecisive. Thus we face not only the paradox but also the pain of mission. We want to be all things to all people, yet we presume to bring something new and challenging; we want to be vulnerable and trusting, yet we do not want to fail to be signs of contradiction. But whatever confusion we ourselves feel, we must surely acknowledge our responsibility to allow our hosts the freedom and the grace to be themselves; to do any less is to fail at a fundamental level.

THE STRANGER AS RECEIVER

Forewarned may be forearmed—or, in our case, disarmed. If we are prepared for being unprepared and unsure and unfamiliar, then we will have
less reason to try to cover our apparent inabilities. We have to learn not
only to accept hospitality and the rest, but that we can only do so *as we go
along*. Hospitality itself is culturally determined and shaped, which means
that we cannot guess beforehand how it operates and what is appropriate
for us. And we *will* be caught unawares by the expectations and habits of
our hosts. So if we are not prepared to learn to modify some of our
attitudes to personal hygiene, privacy, commensality and the rest,[5] then we
remain "unclassifiable" as far as our hosts are concerned, and are not fit
ambassadors of the Jesus who himself came as a willing stranger. But
likewise, unless we have a strong sense of our own personal identity, rooted
yet resilient, we will either compromise totally (which our hosts certainly
do not expect, since part of our attractiveness in their eyes lies precisely in
our quaintness and otherness: our strangeness), or remain enslaved by our
own western habits of dress and demeanor, food and friendship, housing
and hospitality.[6]

A stranger cannot *demand* credibility and legitimation; it is up to the
hosts to *accord* these things, as and when appropriate. But without legitimation—whereby one is "approved" by the authorities as worthy and
respectable— the stranger remains peripheral, distant, and not significant.
The price of legitimation varies. But it may include the passage of time, the
invasion of privacy, the experience of vulnerability, confusion, and some
isolation; and still it ultimately depends, not on the stranger at all, but on
the progress of relationships that would graft the stranger onto the native
stock. The necessary experience of rootlessness, lack of control, and self-
consciousness is also known by a more familiar term: "culture-shock."[7]

THE STRANGER AS RESOURCE

In the contemporary world, some people try to make a virtue of not owing
anything to anyone, being resourceful and self-sufficient, and calling this
attitude "responsible." Carried to its logical conclusion it necessitates
building barriers or fences—physical or ideological or cognitive or whatever—to keep others away and to delimit our own little world. Such an
attitude easily becomes one of xenophobia, distrust and disregard for the

stranger. Some people stoutly maintain that they are justified in not helping others, since the needy are evidently feckless or dishonest. But however foolish this approach is, it is also quite contrary both to cultural and evangelical imperatives. Cultures need outsiders, and the gospel needs to be uttered abroad; otherwise cultures stagnate or are destroyed, and Christians become complacent and selfish.

In a classic work *The Ancient City* (1864), Fustel de Coulanges maintained that ancient cultures always strove to exclude strangers—perhaps with some tribal memory like that of the Trojan horse. But this is clearly not the case; in fact recent work[8] has shown that strangers may actually be necessary for a society to flourish. Already at the level of biological needs, a group must open up and find mates for its womenfolk beyond the available menfolk, and mothers for its children. This leads to some form of self-interested alliances with strangers. But beyond this, strangers have access to other things: other goods, other ideas, other ways of doing things, other techniques, other technologies. The heterogeneity brought by strangers may be necessary to the cultural health and vitality of a group, and the comfortable isolation of a group whose boundaries are always defended against strangers may nurture the seeds of its own decay.

Missionaries are thus potentially life-giving to the people and the cultures they contact. This is already an enormously encouraging fact. But there is more, since missionaries must realize that their own vitality depends on the establishment of reciprocal relationships. If the missionary resists being a stranger, then he or she cannot be accommodated as a stranger is accommodated; and unless the missionary is accommodated, then a culture and a people may have missed a vital opportunity to be enriched and sustained by the resources brought by the missionary. And this takes us back into the heart of our paradox; people need gifts, since gift exchange is life-giving, but unless one is careful of the apparent gift-giver, one may welcome a wolf.

THE STRANGER AS ALIEN

It is very likely that, given the human capacity for setting boundaries and limitations, the stranger at the gate is *primarily* perceived as an alien. After all, such a person does come from "beyond," "the outside," the "over there"; and what is outside the limits of the group tends to be unknown, unfamiliar, and therefore alien. The less known the stranger, or the place from which the stranger comes, the more likelihood that a social group will invest the stranger with bizarre properties and habits, thereby underscoring the dividing line between "one of us" and "one of them." So whatever a group of people may do to transform strangers, if we want to understand the intrinsic status of such persons, we must consider them as aliens.

There are examples of strangers who have never been transformed because the potential hosts have never really engaged in relationships with them. At worst, such strangers are kept at the edges of society and perhaps hounded; at best they may be tolerated and even used in some contractual ways. Yet again we have here situations where strangers are treated as objects *because* perceived as alien, "not-one-of-us"; and how indeed *can* people relate to those they do not acknowledge to be like themselves? The low caste, and particularly the no-caste or outcaste sweepers of India, might be a good case in point. The lower their status the less they can do to make themselves acceptable to higher castes. Like non-indentured slaves they may be used and abused by others, but they are not treated as human beings ("us"); they are treated as aliens ("them").

It does seem rather important that we who consider ourselves benign and compassionate and non-threatening persons should at least consider the perspective of those who place us in the "alien" category, and also the perspective of others who, having been categorized themselves as "aliens" or "strangers," can thus be stripped of their identity and human dignity. It is simply not adequate, or even realistic, for us to expect others to welcome us unequivocally and magnanimously. Those who place us in the "alien" category do so because, for what they deem good reasons, they cannot relate to us and are threatened by us. And those others who have been officially categorized as "aliens" or "strangers" are the stateless persons, the refugees, the shunned, the outcasts, racial minorities, and nearer home those in prison, women in prostitution, addicts of various kinds, and, increasingly, sick, handicapped, and aged persons. If we missionaries have the strength and perhaps the clout to assert our social identity and claim our status, what is the situation of the people just listed? How might our own experience, however mitigated, of being an alien sensitize us to the reality lived out by millions of our contemporaries?

A person who is treated as an alien has the theoretical choice of withdrawing and returning "home." But for many, this is simply not practicable even if possible, and they are reduced to frustration, anger, aggression, or depression and fatalism. Better in many ways, if the alien can be assimilated or positively expelled by the host, than to be left in a liminal, marginal state, to stagnate, and spiritually to die.

In considering the stranger as an alien, there must be many of us whose response is: "not me!"; we do not take easily to being categorized in this way, much less to being judged non-categorizable or unacceptable. But we may have some work to do here. We may have the obligation to learn to live in the transitional state of aliens, and we certainly have to become alerted to the plight of those who live permanently in that condition. Jesus, I think, can teach us these lessons.

The Stranger as Guest

Here we are on more comfortable ground; we can respond well enough to the idea that as strangers we should be treated as guests! But we should be alerted nevertheless to some of the implications here. While one person is being treated as a guest, some of the local community is being deprived; the convenience of the guest is at the expense of the convenience of the community. This is no bad thing; rather it is of the nature of hospitality. But hospitality is not unlimited, and the smiles on the faces of hosts will be strained after a relatively short time. Guests need to learn to read the signs.

Since the guest *is* a stranger, it is not up to him or her to refuse the hospitality; that already smacks of a desire to control! No, the guest must be gracious while learning to be sensitive to nuances that would indicate the approaching end of the welcome period. To approach the role of guest with a patronizing pose or an attitude of self-importance is to insult the host and to demean the process. This is evidently no basis upon which to announce a gospel of service, ministry, and respect for persons.

Strangers, even guests, have no absolute rights; the initiative belongs to the host. To be a guest can be delightful, affirming, and the preamble to developing relationships and mutuality; but it is delicate. And the missionary *must* learn to be a guest not simply as a means to an end, much less as a matter of course. An acceptable guest can be converted by the hosts, to a confidant; a person who fails to convince as a guest will certainly not be worthy of trust in other matters. Jesus, I think, can teach us these lessons.

Assimilation of Strangers

If the host must modify certain attitudes and relationships in order to accommodate the stranger, the latter must undergo a much more demanding modification; the host has at least the "home" advantage, but the stranger is "away" from home. The stranger, then, needs to construct a new pattern of relevance or matrix from the jigsaw puzzle that the hosts seem to be able so effortlessly to solve.

There is a danger, noted by students of this kind of interaction,[9] that the stranger who feels vulnerable may adopt a rigid rather than a relaxed attitude to the hosts, and become serious and tight-lipped rather than jovial and spontaneous. Though certainly understandable, its effect is to mark the stranger as inflexible and rather formal, and thus difficult to assimilate. If assimilation is the ultimate state to which both the stranger and the host aspire, it is nevertheless not easily achieved, since each party is less than sure of the other's expectations and less than clear about the signals he or she transmits.

It may be helpful to consider the three stages of assimilation, classically described by Van Gennep.[10] They are not totally discrete, may not clearly follow one another, and can be subject to variations that cannot easily be specified in advance; but nevertheless, and in their general outline, they can be described as a *preliminary,* a *transitional,* and an *incorporative* stage.

We saw some of the characteristics of the very earliest stages of contact between strangers and their hosts: formality, hesitation and tentativeness, mixed with the desire on the part of the intruder to be accepted, and on the part of the hosts not to be outflanked. Ideally there will be certain "markers" that will indicate clearly to each party the *preliminary* nature of the interaction. There should be some form of introduction, probably preceded by the announcement of the stranger, and there will then be some ritual scrutiny of the incoming person, which may include pointing, touching, stroking, poking, searching, observing, commenting, and perhaps laughter and some apparent humiliation as the stranger is assessed and compared to more familiar points of reference. And there is the waiting, the "time-wasting," the "hanging around," that serves to establish the host as being in charge. The more the stranger is able to tolerate and indeed encourage this kind of behavior, the more likely that he or she will ultimately be assimilated more closely into the group. But it is not always easy, and sometimes very tedious.

As time goes on and assuming the stranger is still being treated sympathetically, attitudes will change. No longer will there be the formal, ceremonial relationships of hospitality and kindness; in fact the stranger may sense a certain cooling-off on the part of the hosts. What was relatively structured behavior in the early stages now becomes frustratingly unpredictable, changeable, even random. And this is a clear indication that the *transitional* or liminal ("threshold") stage is being reached. The incomer is perhaps treated with casualness or even left to manage alone. But the apparent randomness is not random, nor is the casualness casual; the transitional period is, by definition, inconsistent, and of necessity confusing. The stranger is being brought across a threshold, and is neither completely outside (stranger) nor completely within (host). And it is very important that the stranger have the flexibility and the trust and the perseverance to remain committed to the process, rather than allowing the frustration or anger to have full expression. And this may be all very confusing.

Characteristics of the transitional phase include some proffering and acceptance of gifts, some reciprocity and yet no firm committment, some mutual modification of attitude and status between the parties. Neither the stranger nor the guest is entirely happy or comfortable, but neither wishes to abort the process, and each is questioning some basic assumptions, both about self and about the other.

In a sense, the whole of any meeting between two persons or two groups, whether of the same or of different cultures, is transitional, since there is always call for personal and mutual reappraisal, and circumstances may warrant the indefinite delaying of commitments. But in another sense we can say that human associations can mature and pass beyond the liminal phase, as they settle into a committed relationship. And if they do, we can identify the third phase of a social interaction: *incorporation.*

If a person succeeds in achieving incorporation at some level, then the relationship will be characterized by spontaneity and trust, quite a difference from the ambivalence and inconsistency of the liminal phase. But it must be recalled that this is not an inevitable phase: transition may be followed by the breakdown of the relationship. Incorporation certainly depends on mutuality, but the incorporated person is not structurally equal to the host; the host is always superordinate, superior, to the guest. Unless the guest acknowledges this fact by appropriate attitudes, incorporation will not occur. But, more, the incorporated stranger *remains a stranger*, at least for a very, very long time. In Europe a person who moves into a rural village is referred to as a stranger, even after thirty years or more! So what expectations might we reasonably have of being assimilated, at least until we have been with our hosts for several years? And acceptance by the host is no *carte blanche* for the stranger to forget the precedence due to the other. And there is even one more little paradox: if the stranger wishes to remain "free" and not be beholden to the host, then incorporation is not desirable; but where incorporation does take place, then *noblesse oblige* the guest to defer to the host and be loyal rather than critical.

Though we have traveled rapidly through the various stages of interaction between stranger and guest, it should now be possible to address certain questions which are extremely important for us as missionaries. Do we wish to seek incorporation respectfully, or do we demand it? Do we have any understanding of the "grammar" of "stranger-ness"? If we sense that we are incorporated into a group, do we thereby acknowledge our responsibility to support and be loyal to our hosts? Or do we retain our "right" to criticize and judge others, thus effectively making it undesirable for us to seek incorporation?" And what of our hosts: do we appreciate their relative slowness in accepting us fully? Do we understand how seriously they take the duties of hospitality? Can we accept that they remain superordinate, since we are on their turf and not our own? And do we nevertheless aspire to learning how to be appropriate strangers, or do we wish to repudiate the conventions and seize the initiative and control? And what attitudes of Jesus might help us to be more authentic in our approach to other people?

Advantages and Disadvantages of Strangers

It is usually possible to take advantage of a situation, and sometimes it is justifiable. But there are times when such action would be tantamount to unscrupulous self-interest, and missionaries might do well to consider their own motivation as they accept hospitality from local people. One person's advantage may well be another's disadvantage, and opportunity may be one side of a coin whose other side is exploitation.

In a sense, the hosts are imprisoned by their own rules of hospitality. They often react to a stranger with great tolerance and preferential treatment, giving the benefit of the doubt rather than judging too critically. Such an attitude may leave hosts vulnerable to some exploitation by the less-than-scrupulous, or indeed the God-fearing-and-hard-working stranger. But it also provides diligent strangers with opportunity and motivation for advancement, and there are many examples of hosts treating strangers with conscious indulgence, only to find that such strangers rapidly move away from the periphery and toward the center of power and influence. Some of the Chinese who were brought into Hawaii as indentured slaves and laborers in the early nineteenth century achieved, by dint of industry, quiet ambition, support from the extended family, and opportunity, the status of entrepreneurs and politically powerful figures in a couple of generations. Many Pakistani people who moved to England in the past couple of generations became shopkeepers and worked long hours and every day; and some became millionaires. Such upward mobility, while admirable in many ways, may well give pause to hosts, when faced in future by apparently helpless strangers.

It does seem true—but whether this is an advantage or not depends on many variables—that strangers may act as a catalyst for the opening up of societies. From a missionary perspective, such opening-up has been seen as a positive and necessary ingredient of evangelization. But more recently we are becoming aware of the side-effects. This is a delicate and complex issue, beyond our scope here, but one that probably warrants much greater sympathy from missionaries than it has received to date. If you cut a deep furrow with a heavy tractor and plow across the manicured green of a golf course, things will never be the same for the golfers! If the golfers were not consulted, they might be a little put out! If they were informed—as the plow rolled in—that a committee had decided what a good idea it was, they might be forgiven for being somewhat skeptical, not to say disappointed. If they were "persuaded" (bribed) or made signatories to a contract they could not understand, it might be years before confusion turns to resentment. But if they themselves decide that the golf course should give way to kinds of development, they might feel involved in the process and committed to conservation of the totality of the resources.

Strangers are no unmitigated blessing, partly because decisions have to be made in their regard, without all pertinent information. One may regret, a generation later, something done in good faith, but, often, inaction or even delay is not possible: something has to be done when the strangers arrive.

One crucially significant issue is that strangers and hosts are cut off from each other's pasts. They may bond in the present and commit themselves to each other for the future, but they remain strangers to each other's socialization processes, "significant others," and past experience. Perhaps this goes some way to explaining why, very often, people evangelized by "foreign" missionaries never felt they really "belonged" to the church.[12]

Because of divergent pasts, hosts and strangers will always have difficulty in positioning or contextualizing each other. If the stranger clings to the

kind of privacy that seems so essential, then the host will never have
adequate access for the purpose of "positioning" the stranger. If the host
appears too curious or demanding, the stranger may feel that personal
integrity is being impugned. If the stranger is treated with deference and
formality, it will be difficult to perceive the host's real motivations, and
thus may cause discomfort to the sensitive stranger. If the host remains
solicitious and indulgent, then resources may be stretched and the host may
begin to resent the stranger's taking advantage of the demands of hospitality. All in all, then, such is the nature of relationships between strangers and
guests that they tend to preclude real reciprocity, frankness and collaboration. And if the missionary, no less than the host, wishes to build relationships on a more creative footing, then he or she will begin to sense the
inadequacy of the formal relationships and the need to transcend them and
move to something else. But who is to take the initiative here? The host is
unlikely to know what the stranger has in mind; the stranger may sense
resistance from hosts who want to retain their legitimate position of
strength.

Biblical Attitudes to Strangers

Before looking more closely at missionaries—and at Jesus—as strangers, we
might turn to the Bible for information and enlightenment; the Bible after
all is a story full of meetings between strangers and hosts. But since this is
not a piece of biblical scholarship I will be able to do little more than raise a
few points, commend the reader to some real biblical scholarship, and offer
a very brief selection of references. It seems to me that we have here a very
pertinent and rich source of reflection for any missionary trying to understand both service in other cultures and the nature of the missionary task
itself.

Biblically[13] a stranger was someone not a member of the tribe; and as an
outsider the stranger was also seen as an enemy, real or potential. As they
began to develop their own self-consciousness as the chosen people, the
Israelites became concerned about maintaining that identity and not allowing it to be undermined and contaminated by the beliefs and behavior
of strangers; hospitality remained an important virtue and a sign not only of
magnanimity but of urbanity. And when someone was in fact allowed into

the community, that person became *entitled* to hospitality, just as we find today in many other cultures.

It should not surprise us that there was tension where there were strangers; on the one hand the demands of hospitality include indulgence to the stranger, but on the other strangers might well be "unbelievers," "barbarians," "heathens," "pagans." If one categorized the outsider as such, the duties of hospitality might be perceived to conflict with the demands of purity or proselytization.

Strangers were not left in an undifferentiated category, and indeed some movement of status was possible. Of the terms referring to strangers, the one with the strongest negative connotations seems to have been *nokri;* such a one attracted suspicion and hostility. But a stranger could also be a temporary guest, and in fact rise to the status of "permanent resident alien" (*ger*). Indeed, it would seem that in order adequately to understand the call of the chosen people and the nature of the covenant, as well as the existential situation of strangers in biblical times, a study of *ger* is more than desirable, it is necessary. And if, in turn, we are to contextualize ourselves within the culture of others, then we probably need to learn how to be strangers in a strange land ourselves.

The history of the patriarchs is the history of boundaries and transitions, exile and incorporation. Abraham was a stranger (*ger*) in Egypt (Gen 12:10; 17:8; 20:1), as indeed was Moses in Midian (Ex 2:22) and Lot in Sodom (Gen 19:9). So perhaps we should look more closely at this kind of stranger. The *ger* occupied an ambiguous place and enjoyed an uncertain status; such lack of sharp focus was indeed of the nature of a *ger*. Though a *ger* could expect not to be oppressed, and in fact to receive charity (and if necessary, asylum), such a stranger was in no position to *demand* these *as a right*. The *ger* therefore might sometimes be exploited or refused respect, and thus it was advisable to have a protector or a patron. We have already seen the importance of "legitimation" for strangers; the same social mechanism is here uncovered in respect of the stranger.

It was possible, as a stranger (*ger*), to rise to some social prominence, to become wealthy, to possess land; but such a stranger was never assimilated to the very center of society. And we have ourselves seen that the stranger may be accommodated and given protection but should not expect to become pivotal or essential (relevant) except in the most unusual circumstances.

But the story of *ger* goes beyond the cases of individual aliens or outsiders, and becomes something of a theme running right through the history
of the chosen people and on into the mainstream of our own history. Israel
itself was *ger* in a theological sense, existing—settling, dwelling, living,
flourishing—in the land that was Yahweh's land and not a commodity
belonging as "real estate" to the people.[14] Moreover, the individual member
of the chosen people would have been taught to think of himself or herself
as a *ger* of Yahweh, with all the implications of that relationship (Ps 38:13;
118:19). This is critically important, inasmuch as Israel had to learn respect
for and deference toward Yahweh; and we missionaries have to learn to be
strangers in strange lands and to glean appropriate behavior and respect for
our hosts.

When we look at biblical history we cannot fail to be enlightened for our
own journey. And yet it might be argued that, with Jesus, things have
changed: that the Christian is *not ger*. For St. Paul says: "So you are no
longer aliens or foreign visitors; you are citizens like all the saints, and part
of God's household" (Eph 2:19). But McKenzie reminds us that we are
indeed *ger* in reference to "the world"; we have here no abiding city. So the
questions we might put to ourselves include the following: What is the
importance of biblical scholarship and insights for our understanding of the
notion of stranger? Have we spent rather too much time resisting our
identity as stranger in other cultures, and trying to change it? What is the
value of our acknowledging and living out the role and position of stranger
in other cultures? And perhaps the most fundamental: Is it possible to be
truly missionary in the spirit of Jesus *without* undertaking to be strangers?

The Missionary as Stranger

STRANGERS FOR THE SAKE OF THE GOSPEL?

Any missionary is capable of recognizing the features proper to strangers.
And then sensitivity to the feelings of others in situations of transition,
reflection on our own personal feelings in such situations, discussion with
colleagues and with those we meet for the first time, and reading (perhaps
along some of the lines indicated here): all these, along with prayer and
meditation on the work and attitudes of Jesus, may help us identify ourselves as strangers and position ourselves as such.

But there is nothing automatic about this process; in fact there is argu-ably more within us that will resist being categorized and treated as strangers than will equip us for that role and status. It is possible for us to fail to recognize that *we* are the intruder, *we* are perceived as disruptive, *we* probably did not ask permission to invade another world. It is further possible that we are not sensitive to the feelings and needs and rights of others. It is also possible that we discuss our feelings of isolation, culture-shock and ambivalence, neither with colleagues nor with our hosts. And if we are suffering the pains of transition, it is even possible that we find ourselves strangers to prayer and aliens before meditation on the way of our Lord. In short, and in spite of restlessness and frustration, we may simply not notice what is happening to us.

Assuming that we do recognize that we are experiencing a "stranger syndrome," then we are in a position to react to it. We can identify ourselves as marginal, transitional, ambiguous in the lives of our hosts, and we can embrace that status. We can undertake to stray further and further from our own comfortable reference points and trust ourselves to those who live at the margins of our world. We can reflect that Jesus, sent to the outcasts and those on the margins, had of necessity to seek out and find the needy. And we can gather all this knowledge and experience into our prayer, and allow ourselves to be graced as strangers.

And yet . . . such is the strength of our socialization processes and expectations, we may well balk at this challenge. We may identify ourselves, not at all as poor with the poor and weak with the weak and marginalized with the marginalized; we may, implicitly at least, see ourselves as strong, resourceful, independent, pioneering, personal saviors. We may even stop short and refuse to go to seek out and find the needy, expecting them to come to us, and perhaps even thinking we are giving them the initiative in this. The identity of stranger is not an easy one to wear, and missionaries are prone to misunderstand it, misappropriate it, or rebel against it.[15]

Historically, and due to whatever evolutionary, colonial or evangelical perspectives are or were current, missionaries have often reacted strongly to reverse their status as stranger as quickly as possible, demanding to be treated with respect, as guests, celebrities, or even "civilizer" or "God-bringer." Though this was not always so, nor is it today, there does seem to be enough residual confusion on the part of the people to whom we go for us to question the impression that has sometimes been given. Certainly, insofar as the missionary self-image was or is that of giver, initiator, superior, teacher, and so on, at the expense of the reciprocal of each of these, then to that extent we will have failed to learn how to be strangers. And if we decline to be such, what is left of the identity of our hosts?

CURRENT DEVELOPMENTS

From reading and discussion with missionaries, it certainly seems that we are in a period of serious reappraisal of both the missionary task and the missionary relationship with local people and local churches. All that is needed now is for the effects of this reappraisal to be felt by all. We will pursue this topic a little, and then will formulate some more questions relating to ourselves and mission.

If a newcomer honestly presents herself or himself as a stranger, thus showing respect for the hosts and allowing them to take certain necessary initiatives, this facilitates the interaction, even though the price may be some uncertainty and powerlessness on the part of the stranger. But only by doing this will missionaries be able to indicate their openness, integrity, and willingness to engage in relationships.[16]

Intriguingly, missionaries may be their own worst enemies, for it seems that the very qualities that make them adjustable to other cultures (adaptability, initiative, risk-taking, creativity, independence and so on) contain the seeds of problems for their hosts. The latter need to see some dependence, deference, conformity, predictability and so on, on the part of the stranger. So the missionary must live in creative tension, trusting the personal qualities which facilitate survival in other cultures, but listening to the voices and "reading" the expectations and reactions of the hosts in order to adapt, drop defenses, and be able to accept hospitality and all it entails.

I suggest that we missionaries need to work constantly to *accept our marginal and ambiguous status.* We are no longer—if we ever truly were—primary movers, but collaborators and assistants, servants. The primary agent of mission is the Spirit of God; we must not muzzle the Spirit or try to wrest initiatives from God. The primary respondents to God's call are the people; we perhaps need to learn what that may mean as regards our own position. If we try to intercept God's message in the hopes of relaying it to the people, we may badly distort it. If we try to model the only possible and authentic response to the gospel, we will certainly reflect only a shadow of the glory of God. If we presume too quickly to be the mouthpiece of God, we may be overlooking the still, small voice with which God likes to animate the silence. If we patronize and dominate the interaction with other people, they may never gain access to the light so necessary for their own personal growth. Therefore it is good for us to be on the edges, at the margins: for not only does that place us in a position where we may truly co-(l)laborate or co-operate with others, but it allows us to speak directly, to co-(n)verse, co-(l)loquially, together, with others *where they are.*

There needs to be a role-shift; and each of us has to embrace it. We need to work as hard to live out a non-privileged status as our institutional churches have sometimes worked for privilege. We need to relinquish, and sometimes explicitly rather than by default, claims of superiority that were once strident and unsubtle. We must repent and be converted, because we are near to the realm of God (Lk 10:1–9).

There are, close to our own familiar world as well as further afield, many marginal people and marginal castes. Above all others, serious missionaries should be among them, because that is our calling. But if we are to be there it must be with compassion and encouragement and not with triumphalism and threat. We know, but are perhaps not known by and maybe not loved by, abandoned people, abused people, exploited people, condemned people. We are at least aware that our world is populated with refugees, outcasts, prostitutes, prisoners, homeless people. We may be less conscious of how we ourselves contribute to oppression through sexism, consumerism, ageism, clericalism, racism, classism and the rest; and all of these are offenses not just against abstract categories but against real persons loved by God even if not by us. And there is no legitimate escape for us from the marginalized and the needy.

Missionaries, it seems clear, must be in the business of constantly trying to read the signs of the times. "The most abandoned souls of the black race" may have been the honest focus of missionaries a century and a half ago (and still, given modifications in the language, today). But those intervening years have continued to see exploitation and alienation and marginalization on an unprecedented scale, and we must not be impervious to the cries of the poor, however they are identified. How well are missionaries supporting political prisoners, persons in prostitution, those caught in addictive behavior, religious minorities, women? How close are missionaries to (not because we are "good" or "romantic" or "fashionable" or "radical," but because these evils mark the margins where real people are ground down and where real missionaries should be) powerlessness, weakness, statuslessness, poverty, exploitation, homelessness?

To allow oneself to be a stranger is to allow oneself to be placed at the disposition of the God who calls. To embrace the status of a stranger is to empower other people and to dare to infuse some trust into a world where self-interest and suspicion seem to walk unimpeded. To choose to be a stranger is, it might be argued, to be a willing disciple of Jesus.

Jesus, Missionary and Stranger

IMPLICATIONS

Jesus might easily and legitimately have claimed equality with God and played the role of Lord and Savior rather than servant; but "he did not cling to his equality with God, but emptied himself, to assume the condition of a slave, and became as [we] are" (Phil 2:6–7). The condition of a slave is very close to the condition of a stranger waiting on the initiative and indulgence of the host, waiting to be given an identity and some function . . . If Jesus had indeed come as a powerful, high-status, self-important, demanding figure, insisting on his privileged position and the dignity of his office, what respect would that have shown others, and what freedom would it have extended to them?

Sent on an important and urgent mission to the marginalized and victimized, Jesus nevertheless had no home of his own. In fact he had little personal status; the son of a carpenter and a carpenter himself, he was not from the "right family" to make much of a mark. When one of the scribes, mesmerized by the way he spoke, promised enthusiastically to follow him anywhere, Jesus underlined the insecurity of his own lifestyle: "Foxes have lairs and the birds of the air have nests, but the Son of Man has nowhere to lay his head" (Mt 8:20). This evidently impressed the early communities of followers, and the evangelists, and should impress us. Jesus is portrayed as one who showed that he really was a servant, in numerous situations as well as by the whole tenor of his life, his way-of-being-in-the-world. Though not always well-received, he did not "pull rank" or seek out the influential for patronage. He came in openness, and deferentially. To the woman caught in adultery—or prostitution—he was compassionate and "enabling," but to those who claimed to know better and who were hypocritical and harsh, he was uncompromising; yet always he spoke to people in the reality of their lives, not as an airy moralist or doctrinaire theoretician.

When we look at the Jesus of the gospels we can hardly avoid the impression that he deliberately picked the people at the edges, on the margins: the lepers, those living in caves or in the hills, and of course the tax collectors and "sinners." These were the people whom we might identify in contemporary society as people addicted in various ways (alcohol-, food-, drug-, tobacco-, power-, sex-addicts and so on), but also as persons suffering from the effects of the "isms" of the respectable. And this would still leave those persons suffering from handicaps of various kinds (physical, mental, emotional, psychosomatic). Not only did Jesus seek them out and move among them, he took the powerless and empowered them, the withered and regenerated them; he needed them and showed them how important they were; he commissioned them as his witnesses, as the teachers of others, as the media for his message!

It is unquestionably the case that Jesus had nothing to gain in terms of status or reputation from the people he frequented; they simply had nothing to give. Yet he walked with the crippled and talked with the mute, he ate with the starving and drank with the dry. His faith was strengthened by the infidel Syro-phoenician and the Roman soldier, and he was edified by sinners and purified by the ointment of the impure woman. In the heart of paradox and reversal he found and brought clarity and restoration. And for all *our* preparation and rationalization and education and orientation, unless we get to the heart of Jesus and his approach to other people, we will never get to the heart of the gospel or transplant it into any body.[7]

APPLICATIONS

In the spirit of Jesus we must become and be missionary. If it is the case that Jesus came as a stranger and operated as strangers in many societies do, then in the spirit of Jesus we have to become strangers too. I believe that Jesus clearly and deliberately used the potential of his identity as stranger. Who is this man? Can anything good come out of his place? Where does he come from? Come and see:

—Jesus moved, listened, received, shared, adapted; he rejoiced and he wept, he knew when to ask for advice and he was able very simply to give advice. Shouldn't we?

—Jesus shared himself; he shared his time and his energy, his presence and his power, his prayer and his passion. He effectively contextualized himself, incarnated himself, "inculturated" himself. Couldn't we?

—Jesus was able to name his needs. He was so well rooted, psychologically and spiritually, that he was able to claim his need for privacy and prayer, for companionship and consolation. He did not burn himself out in misplaced zeal, but used to withdraw, be alone, go to the hills. Mustn't we?

—Jesus identified and worked with the local community; he picked "unlikely" people to be close to him and carry the responsibility after him. He took pity on the people in general, the crowds around him, and the individuals up in trees or by the roadside. Daren't we?

—Jesus underwent linguistic and cultural adaptation, transition, and assimilation; he used forms of language that engaged and entertained and informed people, telling stories, preaching, spinning parables. He was comprehensible. He used techniques of engagement with his audience: question and answer, dialogue, participation. Don't we?

Jesus was always set for the falling and rising of many; his magnetism saw to that. In whatever he did or said, Jesus never became less than challenging and relevant.[18] Can Jesus, as professional stranger, teach us and inspire us to be more credible preachers-of-the-living-word, more passionate lovers-of-the-unlovely-and-unloved, more servant-like and Christ-like missionaries?

Notes and Bibliography

1. "On Holy Thursday, or Ascension Day, it used to be customary for the parish school children, accompanied by the clergymen and parish officers, to walk through their parish from end to end. The boys were struck with willow wands all along the lines of the boundary. Before maps were common, the boys were thus taught to know the bounds of their own parish. The custom still prevails in some parishes"—*The Dictionary of Phrase and Fable*, E.C. Brewer, Leicester, England, Galley Press, 1988:112.

2. "The domain of King John and his successors in Ireland was marked off, and the part belonging to the English crown was called the *pale*, or the part paled off"—*The Dictionary of Phrase and Fable*, E.C. Brewer, Leicester, England, Galley Press, 1988:932.

3. The classic book to which we refer in the present chapter is Arnold van Gennep's *The Rites of Passage*, London, Routledge, Kegan Paul, 1960/1977. The specific reference here is on page 26.

4. Alfred Schuetz wrote two pertinent articles: "The Stranger," in the *American Journal of Sociology*, 1944:499ff; and "The Homecomer," in the same

journal, 1945:369ff. The distinction between the stranger and the homecomer is extensively developed there. John Dunne in *The Way of All the Earth*, Indiana, Notre Dame, 1972:ix–x, talks in some detail of what he calls the "passing over" and the "coming back." And more recently still, there is an interesting section on the same topic, called "The 'Passing Over' and 'Coming back,' " in Paul Clasper's *Eastern Paths and the Christian Way*, New York, Orbis Press, 1980:122–135.

5. I once arrived, hot and needy, in a remote village in West Africa, having failed to make necessary "provisions." On asking the chief for access to "facilities," I was offered an expansive gesture that embraced the whole horizon over which I had just come. I retraced my steps and found a spot in the primeval forest; but just as I was "committed" to my toilet, I saw a pair of eyes, then another, and another! Clothing myself in my dignity—and the adjacent clothing—and pretending not to be put out, I made my way back to the village. The "eyes" were there before me; everyone was standing waiting for me, laughing and gesticulating in my direction; and among the giggles I heard the gossip being passed with great relish: "he is white *all over*!" It is important for us to "submit" to some such mild indignity, in the cause of allowing ourselves to be "tamed" and contextualized!

6. Bernard-Antoine Joinet produced a pair of very worthy articles in the early 1970s: "I Am a Stranger in My Father's House," in *AFER*, 1972:244ff; and "I Speak in the House of My Hosts," in *Lumen Vitae*, 1974:487ff. I particularly like the first of these, and it certainly contains much helpful material.

7. The term "culture shock" is common enough to be very familiar and easy to read about. Especially helpful might be Denison Nash, "The Ethnologist as Stranger," in *South West Journal of Anthropology*, Volume 19, 1963:149ff.

8. Especially Richard Werbner, "Totemism in History: The Ritual Passage of West African Strangers," *MAN* 14 (4) 1979:663ff.

9. Already referred to is the work by Denison Nash (footnote 7) and Alfred Schuetz (footnote 4); also Georg Simmel's classic work, *The Stranger*, New York, Free Press, 1950.

10. Van Gennep's work is invaluable, not only for the stranger, but for many nuggets of wisdom on rites of passage, the title of his book (note 3). The reference here is to pages 26–38.

11. When I think of missionaries criticizing and judging others on the assumption that their attitudes and approaches are unquestionably correct and the only possible standard for all, I think of the sad way we have created confusion and promoted injustice in relation to marriage patterns and kinship institutions. "Polygamy" is a social institution that has brought down the opposition of missionaries; and yet it is far more complex, nuanced, and capable of inculturating gospel values than most westerners have ever suspected or

allowed. See Eugene Hillman's study, *Polygamy Reconsidered: African Plural Marriage and the Christian Church,* New York, Orbis, 1975, still a sadly neglected or ill-judged piece of work.

12. The standard work on the growing number—over six thousand twenty years ago—of "breakaway" or "separatist" churches in Africa is David Barrett's *Schism and Renewal in Africa: An Analysis of Six Thousand Religious Movements,* Nairobi, Oxford University Press, 1968.

13. Any good Bible dictionary will be immensely helpful as a start. I have used John McKenzie's *Dictionary of the Bible,* New York, Macmillan, 1965:847–849.

14. See Walter Brueggeman, *The Land,* Philadelphia, Fortress Press, 1979.

15. I have looked at "marginality" and the missionary in "Mission as Communication: A Marginal Note," in *Review for Religious,* 43/3 1984:354ff.

16. There are some useful anthropological insights scattered through *Essays on the Ritual of Social Relations* by the late Max Gluckman, Manchester, England, Manchester University Press, 1962.

17. It is my belief that the time has come for us to rework the horticultural metaphor of "transplantation." Culture are not like gardens but more like organisms. We now know enough about organic transplantation to accept that the immune system works *normally* by "rejecting" foreign tissue, unless it can be "persuaded" that such tissues are necessary for its life. Rejection of some missionary approaches, then, is not pathological, but the sign of a struggling and not unhealthy culture.

18. Perhaps Christianity is deemed widely irrelevant today precisely because we have failed to infect people with the living spirit of Jesus and his living words, but have offered a dead text or set of laws. This brings us back to the priority of word over text, gospel over Bible, spirit over letter, spoken of in the previous chapter.

Afterword

There can of course be no conclusion as such, for there is no end to the *Missio Dei,* the mission of God which is liberation and forgiveness and love, and which originates in the creator and courses through created humanity seeking the hearts of all until the end of the ages. Nor is there any conclusion to a book which simply raises questions ever old and ever new. Perhaps such questions may have been couched in a modified or a novel form, but by no means are they answered, much less comprehensively. So there are no conclusions; yet there may be some concluding, some drawing to a close, a provisional and arbitrary termination, that would be appropriate at this point. And perhaps there is also place for a brief recapitulation of some of the underlying rationale.

In the Introduction I addressed the widest possible audience, *all* those trying to live out their Christian vocation and to respond in some fashion to the rallying "Follow me!" of Jesus, and to his great commission to "Go . . . make disciples of all the nations" (Mt 28:19). On an explicit level however, the book may appear to speak to those who uproot themselves and travel far from home to work as "foreign missionaries" in the classical sense. But there should be no real contradiction here, and it has been my intention to dissolve this distinction even though using language which is particularly expressive of the experience of "foreign missionaries'." So the book is indeed addressed to those closer to "home," those who do not travel very far in statute miles, and those who have no reason to think of themselves as "foreign missionaries." And my understanding of "mission," and its use in this book, should form a bridge strong enough to support both the "domestic" and the "foreign" missioner, as well as the traffic generated by Christians of any and every culture, on any and every missionary journey.

If, as I suggested, one of the essential characteristics of mission is "margin," "boundary" or "edge," and another is the dynamic activity of "following," "going," "being sent," "crossing," "reaching," or effecting access or interaction, then it matters little whether the boundaries are at one's feet or ten thousand miles away. What matters is that we have noticed that

139

boundaries serve to hedge about or keep apart, to mark, to isolate or to imprison, and that we have then taken a step, away from the familiar center of our own world, a step across the boundary and out into the unknown. This bold initiative may leave us in "never-never land," "on the edge," "betwixt and between"; or it may project us into a qualitatively different ethos—"another world." If we choose to undertake "marginalization," it is partly because there are already people marginalized perforce, and we feel called, in the spirit of Jesus, to the prophetic role of servant and to the proclamation of a "year of Jubilee" (Lk 4:18–19). If we find ourselves in "another world," it is partly because we have deliberately left the confines of our own. Either way, if our dynamic movement is a response to Jesus—a surge to be disciples and to make disciples (disciples are *mathetes,* "learners") as part of ecclesial communities—then we are authentically involved in mission.

The margins of society are neither deserted nor quiet, but crowded and noisy with the unemployed and the out of work, the homeless and the vagrant, the imprisoned and the unfree, the institutionalized and the abandoned, the abused and the silenced, the humiliated and the ashamed, the hated and the archly pitied: the litany drones like a mantra. But those who live—or simply exist—there cannot be reduced to or dismissed merely as "addicts," "prostitutes," "criminals," "sinners," or even "the poor"; they are not categories or statistics but women and men, flesh and blood, created, redeemed and loved.

Jesus made a preferential option for the people on the margins—"the poor": the dispossessed, the disenfranchised, the despised, the victimized —and to exercise this option he pressed against and broke through and broke down boundaries of every kind. And by breaking down boundaries —of privilege and prejudice—he was able to break through into the lives of the exploited, and to confront status, rank, and person. At every margin or boundary there is the possibility of confrontation with the vulnerability, ignorance, discomfort or fear to be found not only in the situation or in a protagonist, but in ourselves. Now, much of what has been said in *Gifts and Strangers* is by way of suggestion or is only partial, and much more has not been said at all; but throughout it should be possible for us to confront aspects of ourselves as they are mirrored in the conditions described, or in the faces of those who live at or in the margins exposed. And if we respond to the call of Jesus, and find the poor or the constrained or the alienated where we thought our own brothers and sisters lived, then that is as graced a discovery as if we had journeyed to the ends of the earth looking for the poor or the constrained or the alienated, and found in them our lost sisters and brothers.

An evocative title on the pages of old Bibles was "The First—or Second—Book of Paralipomena": the books of the "things left out." In *Gifts and Strangers,* many omissions could be assembled as "paralipomena"; here are three.

The first relates specifically to Roman Catholics in mission. February 24 1969 saw the abolition of *Ius Commissionis;* twenty years on, this seems to be hardly known among the majority of Roman Catholic missionaries whose lives it should have touched and reshaped significantly. *Ius Commissionis* was the right, conferred by Rome and held by various religious orders and institutions of men, of staffing and maintaining and effectively running the dioceses or vicariates—now called "local churches"—in "mission lands," which came under the 1622 Congregation for the Propagation of the Faith. In 1969, however, the local ordinary—normally the bishop of a particular diocese—was constituted fully responsible for the staffing of his own diocese in terms both of "foreign missionaries" and of indigenous ministers, while the religious orders were now required to respond to the requests of local bishops rather than to initiate policy in local churches, and likewise to deploy their personnel, not primarily to support the works that they had come to perceive as their own, but according to the invitations and requests of indigenous bishops in various territories. Before 1969, huge territories had been identified with a particular religious order—and often with one province or national group within that order—which almost invariably saw one of its own members, most commonly an expatriate, as bishop. Now the local bishops, increasingly indigenous to the locality, have the primary responsibility of inviting and deploying clerical and lay assistance from outside, without the previously-held assumption that the communities from which such personnel originate will replace them when necessary. And now the local bishop also carries the responsibility for the financial support of his diocese and its works. Clearly, there has been a crucial shift of resources and executives; yet in practice, many local bishops are often as dependent on the assistance of expatriates—at all levels—as the "foreign missionaries" are notionally dependent on the decisions of the local bishops in respect of placements and policies. A collaborative model might be developing, but where true collaboration demands equal freedom for both parties, there are indications that the future of local churches is still characterized by a dependency that is not always healthy.

If one adds to the developing picture of local churches the relative increase in indigenous ministers in many parts of the world, coupled with the decline in expatriate personnel—at least of the classical, celibate, life-long variety—from Europe and North America, one becomes aware of a monumental, epochal change in the profile of "missions" and "mission-aries" over a couple of decades, the long-term effects of which will be increasingly felt, and, one hopes, creatively addressed by the Roman Catholic Church. And all of this is simply to underline the developing role of local churches and the concomitant dynamic between all those involved. The present book has not followed up this story, but the reader should be aware of it, and, one hopes, find something in the text which can be applied to changing situations in the local churches formerly dependent upon Rome and the individual missionary orders of men.[1]

Secondly, and at least partially related to the abolition of *Ius Commissionis*—but only partially, because those outside the jurisdiction of *Ius Commissionis* already have long experience of the phenomena—is that new forms of service, new kinds of communities, and new understandings of the demands of mission have begun to flourish. Yet it is perhaps not entirely by accident that 1969 also saw the beginnings of what was to become the Volunteer Missionary Movement (VMM) which has recruited and trained and sent more than a thousand young men and women—by no means limited either to Roman Catholics or to celibate "lifers"—to serve in local churches in Africa, Papua New Guinea, and indeed Europe and North America. And, increasingly, opportunities are being made available for all men and women to discover their missionary potential within Christian communities of various kinds. For some, the experience of a couple of years as expatriates in a far-off land is the beginning of a discovery about their role in their own society on their return. For others, typically those originating in what used to be called "mission lands," the discovery of the missionary dimension of their own Christian vocation leads them to the borders or the margins of their own familiar world, and then beyond, into the jungles of modern industrial technocracies. And so "mission" undergoes yet another metamorphosis or transformation—and, again, one that has not been chronicled in the present work. But "mission in reverse" as well as "reverse mission"—people from other cultures crossing over into the improperly-called "first world," and "foreign missionaries" redeploying in marginal situations at the edges of their own cultures—are among the signs of the times that characterize the contemporary era of missions. Again, having chosen to limit the canvas of this book, I hope nevertheless that somewhere in the background or away from the focal point there can be found shadows and echoes that mark the reality of these signs of the times. As it was when St. Paul wrote to the people of Corinth (cf. 1 Cor 12:12–30), so it remains with us, that we are together Christ's body; but each of us is a different part, and we all try to work together harmoniously, in service and collaboration, for the sustaining of the whole organism.

And finally, an explanation or corrective: There are many books available on the theoretical aspects of mission and evangelization,[2] and some on the practical implementation of the injunctions of Jesus. The main purpose of Chapter Five of *Gifts and Strangers* has been to provide a bridge—rickety perhaps, yet temporarily functional and serviceable, one hopes—between the two aspects. Though little more than skeletal at this juncture, it is intended to carry the weight of personal reflection and intentionality, from the plateau of theory to the peak of practice. It will need buttressing and strengthening if much traffic is to use it; but such engineering is largely for the travelers to execute, as they identify the strains and gauge the weight which they, and their respective communities, put upon it. And so I recommend meditation and discussion on Chapter Five, with a view to discovering and sharing more of what it means to be marginal and missionary in the spirit of Jesus and according to our various circumstances. As for myself, I hope to pursue some of its implications in the form of some writing that creates an analogy with Fritz Schumacher's seminal[3] *Small Is Beautiful* where the phrase "appropriate technology" was first employed; I think there is, or should be, an "appropriate spirituality" for missioners that would acknowledge our mobility, impermanence, vulnerability, "strangeness" and "cultural nomadism," and yet our actual incarnation or contextualization, whether in a slum or on a savannah, in a jungle or a geriatric home, on a breadline or in a brothel; for if we go in the name of the Lord, yet hope to find God in the lives of others, rather than to presume to bring God to "Godless" people and places, we must, like Jesus, become all things to all persons; and that, for me, means our appropriating and developing a *variety* of ways-of-being-in-the-world-and-with-God—in short, a variety of "appropriate spiritualities" to sustain us. Inasmuch as this book points out some of the demands of mission, it points out also the need for a spirituality for missionaries. But we have to close somewhere, and it might as well be here.

Notes and Bibliography

1. I refer specifically to religious orders of *men,* since the issue mentioned here was indeed confined to men and did not relate to women. In terms of jurisdiction and canonical authority, religious orders of men carried out the missionary policies of the Roman Catholic Church. Women served, and were indeed not only essential to evangelization in its broadest aspects, but were often more prophetic, fearless, and effective than their male counterparts, as for example the doughty and demanding Mère Anne Marie Javouhey on the West African coast from the second decade of the nineteenth century onward. Yet they did not have the *de iure* authority accorded to the missionary institutes comprised of men.

2. A recent book which provides a comprehensive view of the theology of inculturation, and which can be added to some of those already mentioned, is by Aylward Shorter, *Toward a Theology of Inculturation,* published by Orbis, Maryknoll, 1989.

3. The book is *Small Is Beautiful* by E. F. Schumacher, New York, Harper and Row, 1973.